# The Essential Guide to Geocaching

# The Essential Guide to Geocaching

Tracking Treasure With Your  GPS

## Mike Dyer

Fulcrum Publishing
Golden, Colorado

Library of Congress Cataloging-in-Publication Data
Dyer, Mike, 1977—
  The essential guide to geocaching : tracking treasure with your GPS / Mike Dyer.
      p. cm.
  Includes bibliographical references and index.
  ISBN 1-55591-522-1 (pbk. : alk. paper)
  1. Geocaching (Game) 2. Global Positioning System. I. Title.
  GV1202.G46D94 2004
  623.89—dc22

                              2004012369




Printed in the United States of America
0 9 8 7 6 5 4 3 2 1

Editorial: Katie Raymond, Faith Marcovecchio
Design: Jack Lenzo
Cover image: Jack Lenzo
Cover map courtesy of National Geographic Maps/Trails Illustrated

Fulcrum Publishing
16100 Table Mountain Parkway, Suite 300
Golden, Colorado 80403
(800) 992-2908 • (303) 277-1623
www.fulcrum-books.com

# Table of Contents

# Acknowledgments

A heartfelt thank you goes to my incredible wife, Jessica, for putting up with the many hours I spent on the computer as I wrote this book. In addition, thanks are truly deserved for the support I've received from my good friends Dave Jay, Steve Lownds, Michael Wildschut, and Tammy, Greg, and Woods Deranleau. Thanks to Sam Scinta at Fulcrum Publishing for listening to my idea and believing it would work. Finally, if it wasn't for my mom and dad who encouraged me to work hard, study hard, and play hard from a young age, I may not have gained the knowledge and experience necessary to write this book.

# Introduction

Just 232 years ago, John Hamilton stood before the House of
Commons in London defending his miraculous invention, a
chronometer called Number Four, which served as an accurate tool
for measuring longitude. Mr. Hamilton's Number Four changed the
face of cartography and navigation by enabling accurate measurement of one's position on the Earth. Yet, by modern standards of
accuracy, the 9.6-mile tolerance for error of the seventy-six-pound
Number Four seems incomprehensible. Today the budget-minded
consumer can purchase a palm-sized Global Positioning System
(GPS) receiver for just $100 and achieve accuracy of roughly nine to
fifteen meters (from twenty-seven to forty-five feet).

Having worked in the outdoor industry for more than thirteen
years, I've witnessed firsthand the rapid explosion of consumer-based
GPS technology. I recall selling some of the first consumer-marketed
handheld GPS receivers for outdoor navigation in the mid-'90s.
These relatively large, clumsy, and extremely costly units (approximately $900) had few features and a graphical display no larger
than that of a basic calculator. A select number of individuals began
to embrace the emerging technology, touted as a must-have safety
tool for backcountry navigation. It wasn't but a couple of years before
more feature-laden, smaller, and value-priced units swamped store
shelves and consumers' packs.

Back in 1999, GPS fever gripped the store where I was
employed. Yet many outdoor enthusiasts still did not comprehend
the real advantages of GPS receivers and even fewer actually knew
how to operate their units safely and effectively in order to navigate.
It was at this point that consumers began to purchase GPS receivers
simply because their neighbor had one. But if there was one thing
that made GPS receivers a consumer success, it was the Clinton
administration's order on May 1, 2000, to remove selective availability

(SA), in other words, unscramble GPS system signals. Suddenly, the receiver available at your local specialty shop offered accuracy ten times better than it did just the day before. Units were now accurate enough to pinpoint the location of a small hidden box, not just the parking lot where you left your car. This drastic change in the accuracy of every consumer-based GPS in turn made geocaching possible.

In my experience as part of the outdoor industry I can say I've seen but a few truly new sports or activities emerge and gain popular following: mountain biking, snowboarding, and now, most recently, geocaching. The niche industry that I love has grown tremendously, and while all of these activities have enjoyed a terrific boon, creating new participants and exciting companies and business opportunities, the most important thing they've done is encourage youth to get outdoors. When children participate in outdoor activities they grow healthier, happier, and more confident. In the age of a million distractions it is becoming increasingly challenging for parents to share time with their kids and have their children ask to spend time with them.

My inspiration for this book came from my boss and good friend, Steve Lownds. Steve is blessed with a large family of four daughters, currently ranging in age from their teens to just a little over five. It was when he described a recent challenge of convincing his daughters to participate in an afternoon hike that he revealed the real power of geocaching. After explaining it as a cool game of hide-and-go-seek and showing his daughters how to use a GPS, he set the stage for a weekend "exploration," not just another "boring hike" as they might have called it. After their first successful cache hunt, Steve's daughters will now pick the cache, load the GPS, print out the topos (topographical maps), and restlessly await their next adventure.

This book is designed to provide a broad overview of the phenomenon that is called geocaching. It is tailored to the geocaching novice but designed to educate those more familiar with the game as well. Topics range from the basics of the sport and how to get started to in-depth detail about the various types of cache games to finding and creating your first cache, plus an advanced section on land navigation. Easy step-by-step checklists, a glossary of terms, and a resource listing of manufacturers and organizations related to the sport make this book a handy reference guide.

# Chapter 1
# What Is Geocaching?

Recall your childhood and the school yard games of hide-and-go-seek and scavenger hunts, and the excitement you felt searching for a colored egg on Easter Sunday? Geocaching is all of these games, yet slightly twisted by technology. Instead of seeking out a hiding person or trying to win the game by collecting a set of items, players use a GPS (Global Positioning System) and sometimes additional navigational tools to find a hidden "treasure," known as a geocache. Caches can be as rudimentary as a 35-mm film container filled with scraps of paper serving as a logbook or as elaborate as a plastic tub filled with trinkets and booty.

The premise of geocaching, occasionally referred to as a "stash hunt," is to use a GPS receiver, map, and compass to navigate to the geographic coordinate of the hidden cache. While this may not sound like much of a challenge, finding a well-hidden cache in a forest, meadow, or even an urban setting can take hours of carefully scouring an area not much larger than a three-car garage. Once you have successfully found the cache, the basic rule is to sign the logbook as a means of proving you found it and then return the cache to the exact location in which it was discovered.

Hidden geocache. *(Photograph by Mike Dyer)*

Another aspect of geocaching, which is just as rewarding as finding a cache, is creating your own. Creating a cache allows you to show off your creativity, demonstrate skill as a navigator, and display expertise as a geocacher. There is a great sense of pride in developing a cache that offers a unique challenge. Cache creators are rewarded by hearing about the successes and failures of others who have tried to find their cache and solve any associated riddles. Creating a geocache is as much about choosing the perfect location as it is about developing new twists and turns that keep the game growing. Expert cache creators build a reputation based on the difficulty and creativeness of their hidden treasure.

Geocaching is nothing more complicated than hide-and-go-seek for a technologically endowed audience. While there isn't any data to support this claim, my guess is that the average geocacher is in his or her mid-thirties, considered techno savvy, outdoor oriented, and enjoys solving problems and seeking adventure. Mastering geocaching is not difficult and no one should fear getting started, yet someone new to the outdoors and, especially, new to GPS receivers and land navigation will certainly benefit from the forthcoming chapters and some hands-on experience. After a couple of successful and unsuccessful cache trips, you'll be well on your way to becoming an expert at this up-and-coming sport.

## A Brief History of Geocaching

Geocaching's history is symbiotic to that of the GPS and the later advent of consumer-based GPS receivers. GPS technology was developed and first employed by the Department of Defense (DoD) in the early '80s. The system was designed to replace previous radio-based methods of navigation for sea and air travel. The vision was that a constellation of satellites could provide a means of triangulating a position on Earth with incredible accuracy that would not be affected by weather or location and only required a clear view of the sky. As GPS satellites were put into orbit, the decision was made to allow civilian companies access to the frequencies of data projected by the satellites, but, for national security reasons, the data would be "watered down" with a slight inaccuracy. This degradation of the signal was referred to as selective availability (SA), and it meant that civilian receivers had accuracies of roughly 100 meters, or 300 feet, compared to the one-foot accuracy of government systems, which were not affected by SA. This inaccuracy certainly made GPS receivers useful for consumer needs, such as finding your way to a lake or to the parking lot where you left your car at the trailhead, but it was not accurate enough to find a hidden geocache.

Civilian GPS units really began to take off in the mid-'90s. A variety of manufacturers such as Garmin and Magellan led the way with the first affordable units that contained features an outdoor enthusiast would enjoy, features such as simple, easy-to-read menus, outdoor-oriented icons, and small, robust, packable designs. From the media and colleagues, consumers began to hear more and more about the benefits of GPS receivers as a safety tool, as a convenience, and as a wonderful recorder of your outdoor trips and adventures. And while these newly added features—as well as marketing by manufacturers—increased sales, the real boon for GPS receivers came on May 1, 2000, when President Clinton removed SA and thereby increased the accuracy of every GPS on the market to approximately nine to fifteen meters. This single act not only made geocaching possible, it enabled GPS technology to take on a new life as a highly accurate navigational tool for everyone. Chances are that the car you looked at in the showroom this past weekend has a built-in navigational system, complete with street maps and routing capability for anywhere in North America. If SA were still in place today, a GPS embedded in the car would not be accurate enough to know which side of a street you were on, or when a turn was approaching. In addition to our cars, nearly all commercial and private planes now rely on GPS as a key means of navigating our skies and directing aircraft to the appropriate runway. The same goes for boating enthusiasts, whether they are using GPS to navigate a complex set of channels such as in the San Francisco Bay or merely to work their way to a favorite bonefishing location in an estuary near New Orleans. Although GPS receivers were good with SA, they became incredible assets and conveniences when SA was removed.

Geocaching, therefore, became feasible on May 1, 2000, and within two days the first documented geocache was hidden outside Portland, Oregon, in celebration of the improved GPS accuracy. Mike Teague is considered the creator of the sport. Not only was he one of the first to successfully locate the original stash, but, more importantly, he developed the original geocache newsgroup by organizing the first Web site to share and track information regarding caches. Of course, the concept of a hide-and-go-seek game using navigational tools is nothing new. In fact, as a means of testing our navigational skills my college surveying professor made several quizzes that involved finding a particular benchmark or hidden "cache." But these games, prior to the accessibility of GPS, relied on orienteering and map reading rather than GPS technology. Geocaching was truly a new sport supported by the growing worldwide acceptance of the Internet and now highly accurate, affordable GPS receivers.

Just a few months later, in July 2000, the sport was beginning to spread and Jeremy Irish had just experienced geocaching for the first time. While Mike Teague was the organizing factor behind geocaching, Jeremy Irish had the vision needed in order to make the sport grow. That summer, Irish approached Teague with a robust design for a new Web site and coined the term "geocaching." Geocaching.com, now recognized as *the* Web site for the sport, was launched in the fall of 2000 with superior functionality and ease of use to support the growing activity. To this day, Irish is still very involved with the sport and is a founding partner of Groundspeak, which owns and operates the Geocaching.com Web site.

Over the past three years the game has grown by leaps and bounds, now with worldwide participation. Caches are being created at the astonishing rate of more than 5,000 per month, which means there must certainly be a greater number of participants. Geocaching is on the cusp of a major growth spurt, fueled by the realization from outdoor retailers and manufacturers of its significance. While researching material for this book, I contacted a variety of both types of companies and heard a common theme of "We're really interested in geocaching and have made it a priority this year." Equipment manufacturers such as Garmin, for example, have started to build features into their products that are exclusively for geocaching. The new Garmin 60CS has treasure box icons to show caches, and National Geographic's State Series topographic mapping software will support the direct download of cache information from the Web.

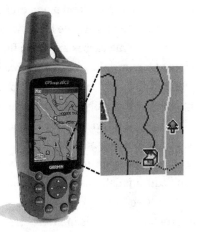

Garmin 60CS. Note the treasure box icons on the unit's screen, which represent geocaches. *(Courtesy of Garmin)*

For those of you who are new to the sport, you couldn't have picked a better time to begin. The number of caches already hidden worldwide ensures that the game must be fun, and the numbers are growing weekly to keep the game exciting and challenging. The added level of participation from key retailers and manufacturers, improvements in technology, and the availability of specialized equipment for our sport will continue to encourage more people to join in the fun.

## Who Should Get Involved in Geocaching?

Geocaching does not require any extraordinary physical or mental capabilities. Therefore, no one is excluded from actively participating in the sport and being successful at it. The combinations of navigational skills with outdoor exercise (which can include many activities, from hiking to mountain biking to paddling) are a great way to improve your well-being and relieve stress. A day of geocaching doesn't require a particular pace, and many caches can be found in local parks or other readily accessible areas, in many cases even for those with disabilities. Some caches are just a few yards from driving access, while others may be in more remote locations that require a greater commitment of time and exertion. There are even caches hidden in places such as public malls, libraries, and on city streets for those who either don't want to tempt poor weather conditions or are not fond of *too* much nature.

There are several groups of people who find geocaching not only fun but also beneficial and educational. The first and most beneficially influenced group is children. Geocaching can be a great learning activity for children, improving their skills in math, critical thinking, geography, and outdoor awareness, all through the guise of a "treasure hunt." Often these subjects, and in many cases anything educational, are not captivating. But what child doesn't want to play hide-and-go-seek or go on a treasure hunt? It is astounding the number of high school students, or even adults for that matter, who cannot answer simple geography questions. The National Geographic–Roper 2002 Global Geographic Literacy Survey revealed that only 17 percent of young American adults could find Afghanistan on a map and that more young adults could tell you that *Survivor* takes place in the Pearl Islands off of Panama than describe the location of Israel. This is a problem too big to be solved by geocaching, but making geography fun at any age is a great way to start.

Along those same lines, we, as U.S. citizens, are bombarded by reports and statistics regarding the unhealthy lives our children are leading. Playing outdoors has become second-best to video games and TV, leading to obesity and even affecting kids' ability to simply fight off an oncoming cold. In my neighborhood there are a lot of kids, yet rarely do I see them playing ball, riding bikes, or running around after school. It is difficult to compete with the cartoon superheroes, but a fun game of geocaching may be an answer. It is important to remember that geocaching doesn't need to be a desti-nation event. A baseball field or playground in your neighborhood can serve as the spot for a hidden geocache. Parents seeking a fun game at a child's birthday party, for example, could hide a cache in the backyard or at a local park. And certainly a group of friends could challenge each other with their own cache games, assuming their parents agree to let them use the GPS.

A friend of mine has a young son named Liam. Recently, Dave told me a story about a day trip he and Liam were on. They came upon a gentleman who told them of an old mine in the area. Dave, being a map buff, had found the mine on a USGS topo and decided that a great hike and event for the two of them would be to find the "lost" mine. As Dave described it, "Liam was fired up! We hiked for hours, scrambling and searching without one whimper or complaint from Liam, just pure enthusiasm for finding the 'lost' mine." When they did find it, Liam was ecstatic. Yet, as Dave points out, just a weekend later he had hoped to go on a short, two-mile hike with Liam but after only twenty minutes of walking, Liam complained, "... my ankles hurt. Dad, can we go back? I wanna go home, this is boring, carry me!" With the focus of finding the "lost" mine gone, Liam ended up like most other children. Clearly, geocaching has an advantage of being able to motivate young children with a fun and adventurous sport that takes their minds off of the hike and exercise and disguises the education they are unknowingly absorbing.

Geocaching is also an appropriate activity for the Boy and Girl Scouts of America. As an Eagle Scout, I loved my time in Boy Scouts and know that I learned a lot about self-discipline, the outdoors, and character in the few short years that scouting was a part of my life. I couldn't imagine a better game than geocaching for a scout trip. Learning how to use a map, compass, and GPS together can be either a lot of fun or very tedious. By teaching and reinforcing these skills via geocaching, the kids will focus on the object of the game and will learn without struggle or reluctance. Creating a troop geocache for an upcoming jamboree or other event would be a great way to propel your land navigational skills forward and have a great time.

Enjoying the outdoors in any form is a cornerstone of learning about yourself, strengthening your mind and body, and growing up. Several nonprofit organizations, such as Big City Mountaineers, are in the practice of leading inner city youth on weeklong backpacking trips as a way of building character, achieving goals, and building self-confidence. But, mainly as a result of television, video games, and other technological and societal distractions, fewer children will take part in outdoor activities this year than the year before—truly a shame and a problem that society should address. Those of us who are passionate about the outdoors should continue to think of new

ways to encourage younger generations to find the freedom, enjoyment, and fun that comes from spending time in nature. Games such
as geocaching—or exciting and unique sports such as dirt-boarding,
kite-skiing, and jibbing—improve kids' lives by encouraging a
healthy and active lifestyle.

But geocaching is not only for children; there are large numbers
of adults who have embraced the idea of leading a more outdoor-
oriented life but are still learning how navigation fits into the bigger
picture. There are many moms and dads, for example, who received
GPS receivers as a present—because you need one to go outdoors,
right? Then there are the "gear-heads," those who have to have the
lightest backpack, the sleekest tent, and all the latest equipment.
And there is a small group of enthusiasts who have decided that
they want a GPS receiver simply because they want to participate in
geocaching. This last group is actually very diverse, ranging from
twenty-somethings who are eager to be on the cutting edge of a new
trend to a large population of retirees who are searching for a way to
maintain a healthy and active lifestyle while participating in a sport
that can be enjoyed at a leisurely pace nationwide. For all of these
groups, geocaching is once again the answer. Getting involved in the
sport will not only help you make sense of your GPS receiver, it will
also help you meet your personal goals and needs. This segment of
the population can hereby label themselves "Generation GPS."

A lot of GPS books are on the market. Some are very good, but
in my opinion all of them are kind of heavy and haven't quite made
my GPS "come alive." This is not to say that these are not valuable
books—you'll learn a lot about GPS technology and how it works,
coordinating systems, datums, and all kinds of other detailed geographic information. But for those of you who do not have a degree
in geography, these books may do nothing but make the GPS seem
like a more daunting tool. Much of this information is very important and we'll cover some of these topics—the basics—throughout

the book. But where geocaching really shines for Generation GPS is in its ability to teach us how to use a GPS, map, and compass *without thinking about it*.

If you can relate to the following experience, then I guarantee that becoming involved in geocaching will be worthwhile:

> You got your new GPS, popped the batteries in, and walked outside. After a couple minutes the screen changed and a set of very long numbers with little fluctuating bars at the bottom appeared. "Great, honey," you exclaim, "I found our house!"

GPS receivers are useful, but unless you understand their functionality and limitations, and also know how to use them properly, you could end up in a dangerous situation and in a world of hurt, or simply get frustrated and put yours away.

Geocaching will teach you how to read a map, how to enter a destination into your GPS, how to use it effectively, and how to navigate in conjunction with a compass and map seamlessly and effortlessly. The concepts that you and your children will learn from the sport will then apply to all of your outdoor trip planning. As a family you will become navigation experts, more aware of the outdoors while at the same time instilling some wonder in geography.

## Where Is Geocaching Today?

More than 90,000 geocaches could be found in at least 190 countries and all 50 United States at the time this page was written. The sport has come a long way in the short four years since the first cache was hidden in the Pacific Northwest. There are geocaching clubs in almost every country, and a wide variety of local clubs and organizations have sprung up closer to home as well. Caches are even being set up as company team-building exercises, similar to the rope courses and climbing events that have also become popular. The sport has grown from its quasi "cultlike" roots to a marketed and accepted outdoor activity, complete with retailers that stock "geocache-ready" equipment manufactured by a new segment of outdoor vendors. Geocaching is envisioned as a growth segment of their business, and retailers are beginning to cater to the unique needs of the geocacher as a distinct market.

Geocaching.com is certainly the hub for the sport. It is the main repository for cache locations, official geocache supplies, and dissemination of the sport's rules and guidelines. In addition to this Web site, various other online newsgroups, clubs, and assorted organizations are also hosting their own lists of caches, and I'm sure that there are off-line clubs as well. While not yet common, I foresee many navigational equipment companies, nonprofit outdoor organizations, and outdoor retailers beginning to create their own sponsored caches and hosting geocache information on their own Web sites. Geocaching has spread far beyond what many would have imagined and continues to reinvent itself through its creative participants. But regardless of its short-term success, the sport is still young enough that if you ask most people on the street what geocaching is, you'll likely get blank stares. Its popularity is growing rapidly but still includes only a very small percentage of the total population of outdoor participants.

# Chapter 2
## Getting Started

### Tools of the Trade

Before participating in your first geocache hunt you need a few specific pieces of equipment. At a bare minimum you'll need a GPS, map of the area you are going to, a basic compass, and coordinates to the hidden cache. While the act of finding a cache does not require a computer and Internet access, your options for discovering new caches and participating in all the varying aspects of the game will be limited without it. To help you get started with acquiring what you need, in the next few pages we'll break down some of the options available to you in the marketplace today. If you already have your GPS, I suggest reading through the sections on compasses and maps. While you certainly do not need all the latest gadgets to participate in geocaching, there are some products that can make your experience more enjoyable and aid in developing better caches on your own. Someone without any navigational equipment can acquire everything he or she needs to participate for less than $200, with a GPS receiver representing half the total expense. Compared to many outdoor activities such as backpacking, fly-fishing, or climbing, this is a significantly smaller investment in the gear needed to get started.

A few Garmin and Suunto X9 GPS receivers. *(Courtesy of Garmin and Suunto)*

## GPS Receivers

As I remarked earlier, GPS technology was originally developed for the military as a means of accurately navigating across the globe through all types of adverse weather conditions and terrains. We, as consumers, have reaped the benefit from this military funding, for we now have an indispensable tool for navigation, whether it is on trail, by sea, or in our car.

When it comes to GPS receivers for geocaching, it is important to remember one thing: at the consumer level, not one GPS receiver is significantly more accurate than another. There are highly accurate GPS receivers designed for surveying and military applications, but they are certainly not intended for our purposes nor meet our price range. The distinguishing factors between one consumer-level GPS versus another come down to their features, hardware technology, and finally their cost, with prices ranging from roughly $100 to $600 for units that are best suited to the rigors of geocaching.

Myriad options are available in GPS receivers today, yet all units offer the same basic functionality of telling you where you are, in the form of a geographic coordinate, and directing you to another geographic coordinate, for example the position of a geocache. Before purchasing any GPS it is important to understand the fundamentals of how the receivers function, regardless of feature set or price.

A GPS receiver interprets signals broadcast by the constellation of satellites high above the Earth. In order to calculate your position, a GPS needs to receive a signal from at least three satellites, but can provide more accurate positions with more. This is why accuracy of any GPS can fluctuate; it is greatly affected by things such as tree cover, terrain, or being on a street among skyscrapers. Once a GPS has "acquired" your location, it will display it in your choice of hundreds of different coordinate systems and mapping datums. Simply put, these are coordinates such as latitude and longitude or Universal

Transverse Mercators (UTM), which are probably more familiar. A receiver can then calculate which direction you need to head in order to arrive at your desired destination, as long as you provide it with the coordinate for that location. However, GPS receivers function by providing you with "as-the-crow-flies," or straight-line, directions, which are often impractical for overland travel.

I like to use the following example to visualize how GPS receivers work:

> You are standing at Curry Village in the heart of Yosemite Valley. It is a bright, beautiful day and you are going to hike to the top of Half Dome. You turn on your trusty GPS receiver and enter the coordinate for the summit. The GPS quickly displays an arrow on the screen, directing you in the shortest straight-line distance between your current location and your destination, in this case directly up the sheer face of Half Dome!

While this certainly would be an exciting way to get to the top, it is probably not realistic for most of us.

GPS receivers offer point "A" to point "B" directions, always showing the shortest straight path between two points and never accounting for things such as terrain, impassable streams, or cliffs. To overcome this challenge, people navigate with GPS units using a string of coordinates to reach their destination, often known as a route. In my Yosemite example, there might be twenty key intersections of trails or major changes in direction that I'd enter into my GPS as one contiguous path. The GPS would then direct me from the start to the next point and so on until I reached my final destination. In geocaching you are presented with the coordinate of the cache hiding place but will often need to add other coordinates along the way, such as where to park, trail junctions, and the spot at which to leave the trail to search for the cache.

All GPS receivers offer the basic functionality described above—of leading you from one place to another—so the variation in price among units is entirely dependent on additional features layered into the device. When beginning the selection process for a GPS receiver, understanding your needs will help you quickly sort through the staggering number of models and make the process seem less complex. To do this, evaluate the following:

- Do I need my GPS to display maps?
- What type of terrain do I intend to use my GPS in most frequently?
- Is size and weight a critical concern?
- What is my budget?

**Do I need my GPS to display maps?**

The incorporation of map databases into GPS receivers is the main distinction among different types of receivers today. The type and detail of the maps available on units vary depending on the amount of memory the receiver has and range from a road atlas to topographical map data. If you envision yourself using your GPS for an upcoming cross-country road trip, then having a basic map of the United States would be extremely helpful. Not only are major roads depicted, some high-end units include points of interest and facilities at each highway exit. These features could be very helpful to someone who travels frequently for business. On the other hand, the topographical data on receivers continues to improve each year and for geocaching or other outdoor activities this can be a great aid in understanding your relative position on the ground and visualizing terrain ahead.

But keep in mind that while additional map databases are certainly nice to have, they are not *necessary* to participate in geocaching. Since most consumer-based GPS units have a relatively small screen— just a couple of inches in size—the amount of map area that can be displayed at any one time is significantly smaller than any printed map, even one printed from a home computer on paper that is eight and a half by eleven inches. Screen resolution and memory capability in these units is increasing rapidly and has made the map information far more readable and useful in just the past few years. But be aware that a map on a GPS is nowhere near as useful or as safe as a printed map. It is impossible to take a bearing, triangulate your position, or understand the broad shape of the land around you from even the largest GPS unit screens.

If you've decided that maps would be useful for your needs, the following models have some of the best screen resolutions and map capabilities available on the market today: Garmin 60C, 60CS, 76, 76S; and Magellan Meridian Series.

Garmin Ique and Garmin 60CS. One of the greatest distinctions among GPS units on the market today is whether or not they offer built-in map databases. (*Courtesy of Garmin*)

**What type of terrain do I intend to use my GPS in most frequently?**
Hardware technology varies by manufacturer and certainly among models. One of the latest developments in receivers is advanced antenna technology. Some newer antennas can clearly filter signals in very dense tree cover or narrow canyons better than the basic

patch antennas found in most units. If you live in an area with dense forest, such as the Appalachians, for example, or if you plan on doing a fair amount of canyoneering, then investing the extra money for a receiver with a more robust antenna may be of great benefit to you. You may also see that some receivers are Wide Area Augmentation System (WAAS) enabled. WAAS incorporates a set of ground-based GPS towers to the satellite constellation. It improves accuracy of your GPS by up to five times and does not add any additional usage cost.

Another consideration is how much water your GPS can withstand. Select units are "dunk-proof." Not to imply that you can go diving with them or place them underwater for a prolonged period of time, but certainly they can be briefly submerged and can stand up to rain and snow without any issues. If you are in an area that receives a lot of precipitation or you will often be traversing streams, you should consider this feature.

Units that integrate altimeters and digital compasses are becoming increasingly common. In states such as Colorado, having an altimeter can be a useful and fun tool for tracking total vertical gain, as well as monitoring barometric pressure in anticipation of changing weather conditions on a prolonged trip. But in Kansas the ability to track vertical gain may be a waste of money. The digital compass is a very useful feature to have on a GPS receiver (though I'll stress that you should always carry a traditional compass with you in case your GPS dies). A built-in compass overcomes a basic inadequacy with all GPS receivers: its ability to point you in the correct direction of travel when you are not moving. Since a GPS only knows at what *point* on the Earth you are, it cannot tell which *direction* you are facing, and therefore can only point you where to go when moving. But a GPS with an integrated digital compass can tell which way you are facing, and, when you are standing still, it will continue to accurately direct you toward your destination. Of all the features out there today, the digital compass is one of the most useful,

especially for geocaching, which often involves starting and stopping and spending a lot of time in one spot while looking for a hidden cache. Some of the more popular models that include these terrain-specific features are the Garmin 60CS and 76, Rino 130, Geko 301, eTrex Vista, and Summit.

Some GPS models, such as the Garmin Rino pictured here, include added features such as built-in family radio service (FRS), while other units, such as the Geko 301, include altimeters and digital compasses. *(Courtesy of Garmin)*

**Is size and weight a critical concern?**
For many people GPS size and weight are relative; if the unit they are evaluating is a "tank," they may want something smaller. But for others, such as an ultralight backpacker or someone planning a long-distance trek, there may be very specific requirements as to the dimension and weight of the receiver they can carry. There are some very tiny receivers on the market today. The Garmin Geko series, for

example, is about the size of a small flip-phone (roughly two inches by four inches). But currently, Suunto has everyone beat on size with their new X9 wrist-top computer, which incorporates fully featured GPS technology, a digital compass, altimeter, and a slew of other features into a large watch. Yet, for most of us, having a tiny receiver is not a necessity. I'd encourage you to go to your local retailer and physically hold a variety of units before purchasing one. If you have small hands, like I do, most receivers won't be a challenge to use, but some units have rather small screens that may be harder to read for those with weaker eyes. Find a unit that has a comfortable design and is easy to read. This should be your guide for size unless you are very concerned about meeting specific needs.

If size is a critical concern, then few GPS receivers can match the size and functionality of the Suunto X9. *(Courtesy of Suunto)*

### What is my budget?

I've decided to make the final consideration price, not because I want you to buy more than you need, but because I want you to understand all of your options before taking price into account. Unlike any of the other considerations, price is *the* deal breaker of the purchase and should be used to sort what features you really need and what you'd *like* to have. GPS units range in price from

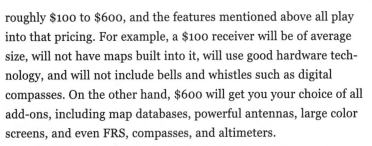

roughly $100 to $600, and the features mentioned above all play into that pricing. For example, a $100 receiver will be of average size, will not have maps built into it, will use good hardware technology, and will not include bells and whistles such as digital compasses. On the other hand, $600 will get you your choice of all add-ons, including map databases, powerful antennas, large color screens, and even FRS, compasses, and altimeters.

All GPS receivers include the basic functions necessary to participate in geocaching, and there are no additional features that will likely make you any more successful. If you are new to GPS and are looking to get started, I'd suggest a receiver such as a Garmin eTrex GPS 12 or a Garmin Geko, both of which will work just fine and get you to as many caches as a significantly more expensive unit will. For those who want a more feature-packed unit, I'd evaluate the Garmin 60 and 76 series units, which have amazing screens; the Suunto X9, for its miniscule size and depth of features; and finally the eTrek Summit and Legend and the Garmin Geko 301. I religiously use my Garmin 12 for geocaching versus the more expensive units in my repertoire because of its simple layout and easy functionality. Any way you slice it—basic or advanced—all GPS units will get you into geocaching and enable you to have a lot of fun and great success.

## GPS Accessories

When purchasing your GPS, a slew of accessories will be presented to you as well. None of the accessories are necessary in order to use your GPS or to participate in geocaching, but there are several that will make your new GPS more functionally friendly. A computer connection cable (usually a serial cable, but some models now offer USB) opens up an immense amount of functionality. Most upper-echelon units will likely include the cable with the unit, but for the entry-level units this may be up to an additional $30 investment. The connectivity cable enables you to upload and download the saved waypoints, tracks, and routes from your GPS unit to software applications designed for managing this data. Computers offer seemingly infinite storage for this type of data, compared with the relatively limited storage capabilities of most GPS receivers. By saving this data to your PC you retain all those great places, hikes, and rides, and can reload them for future use. Frankly, GPS units are not great at manually loading data. None of them have a keyboard so imputing a coordinate requires hitting the same key repeatedly to get to one number or letter, similar to text messaging on your cell phone. The connectivity cable will also open up a world of mapping software, such as those made by National Geographic, DeLorme, and Maptech, from which you can plan your cache hunts, design other trips, and record your outdoor experiences in a journal-like format.

In addition to the cable I would invest in a sturdy, padded case for your receiver. All GPS manufacturers make cases designed for their various models, but there is a wide variety of third-party products as well. Find one that meets your needs, but definitely protect your GPS receiver from getting beat up in a glove compartment or from loose change and spare batteries in the bottom of your backpack.

If you plan on using your GPS in your car or on your bike there are many mounts available to make this easier, including handlebar and dash mounts. Since most geocaching is done on foot you won't need these items to get going, but, once again, if you're looking to accessorize your new toy there are lots of goodies to consider, either at the time of purchase or in the future.

## Compasses

There are three main types of compasses: baseplate
(Suunto GPS Plotter), lensatic (Brunton 9075), and
mirrored (Suunto MC-2), as shown here. *(Courtesy of
Brunton and Suunto)*

"What can I learn about a compass?" you must be asking yourself,
seeing the title of this section. They all point to magnetic north,
right? Well, yes. The main point of this section is to drive home the
need for you to carry a backup navigational device to your GPS, and
the compass is it.

I can list a variety of reasons your GPS could stop working,
ranging from dead batteries to dropping the unit and breaking the
screen to simply not being able to receive signals due to poor sky
visibility. But the essential reason why you should have a compass is
to be prepared. In the past ten years I've had two GPS receivers
conk out in the field for various reasons. In both cases it was more

frustrating than dangerous, but, as in many parts of life, beware of Murphy's Law.

Several different types of compasses should be considered. The price range for all of them is from $20 to $100, and for our discussion I'm not including any compasses that are part of another item, i.e. embedded on a key fob, part of your pocketknife, on the end of your walking stick, etc. While those *are* compasses, they are not designed for any kind of reliable navigation and are more of an accessory (but would make a great trinket to drop in a cache you find).

Baseplate, lensatic, and mirrored are the three main types of compasses to consider (excluded from this list are professional models often referred to as transits). Baseplate compasses are incredible tools for working with a printed map or chart. This makes them ideal for planning purposes and helpful for interpreting the land in terms of distance, reading coordinates, and finding bearings. The baseplate, from which this compass derives its name, is usually made of a clear plastic material with a variety of handy scale tools and coordinate grid information embedded into it. Baseplate models typically do not have a sight for aligning with distant, real-world objects but can still be used effectively to navigate long distances over land. Although they appear to be "lesser" units, baseplate compasses are by no means basic; they are incredibly useful when working with maps and are sufficient for backcountry navigation. There are several baseplate models marketed as GPS compasses, which may be a little deceiving. These compasses have a few extra grid tools and conversion scales built into the baseplate making it easier to find a coordinate on a paper map, but they are certainly not GPS receivers. Some popular baseplate models on the market today are the Suunto A20, A30, and M2 along with the Brunton 54LU Combi, 8096 Eclipse, and the 3DLU Expedition.

The second type, lensatic compasses, do not have a baseplate for easy alignment and planning with a map; they do, however, have a sight and a retractable lens designed specifically to take a bearing off of a distant object. Lensatic compasses will be more efficient than baseplate models at navigating point to point, but they are not especially useful for planning purposes and are not as common as baseplate or mirrored compasses. For geocaching, a lensatic compass would work just fine for verifying a direction to a cache when stopped with a GPS and would allow you to take a more accurate bearing to a distant feature. Some popular lensatic models are the Brunton 9075 and 9076 models.

Finally, some compasses are mirrored. Mirrored compasses are highly accurate by design, achieving readings of less than one degree while utilizing their ability to sight off of an object and simultaneously align the magnetic needle and orienting arrows to take a precision bearing. Many quality mirrored compasses also include a featured baseplate, which makes them useful for map work and planning purposes in addition to field navigation. Fully featured mirrored compasses can be expensive, with the most costly versions approaching $100. My suggested model is the Suunto MC-2D, which will meet all of your compass needs, but other quality models include the Suunto MCA and MCB, and the Brunton Safari, 8040G Classic, the innovative 8099 Eclipse, and Eclipse Pro.

Out of these three types of compasses I prefer the mirrored units due to their accuracy and flexibility in terms of functionality. When choosing a mirrored compass I would ensure that it has a read-through baseplate with an array of scales, and conversion tools for working with printed maps. Much of the planning in geocaching involves developing a route for reaching the cache. Since most games simply supply a coordinate to a location you must plan the most efficient route to get there with the least amount of environmental impact and personal strain. A compass with a baseplate will aid significantly throughout this process, enabling you to use its tools to find coordinates easily and calculate distances and bearings effortlessly. Once in the field, the sighting mirror will make it easier to stay on course and verify your location through resection more accurately than a baseplate model alone.

As with GPS receivers, there are a variety of compass manufacturers and models to choose from. Some of the most respected names in compasses are Brunton and Suunto, and their products can be found at any major outdoor retailer. A good compass will last for years, and many include lifetime warranties on craftsmanship and accuracy. A geocacher doesn't need the most expensive compass on the market, but as your skill as a navigator grows you'll appreciate the quality you invest in.

## Maps

When produced to high standards a map is unlike any other product in the world: it has the incredible ability to put a piece of the Earth in our hands for easy interpretation. Successful geocaching relies on having a quality map, not solely for safety, but, more significantly, for planning your route. A good road map and a topographic map are essential for successful geocaching. Map technology has changed greatly over the past few years, and we are now blessed with abundant sources of both digital and traditional sources of cartographic information.

Traditional cartography is defined as any physically printed, published, and mass-produced map. Traditional cartography ranges from a road map of your town to an updated trail map of your local park to large wall maps of the world and beautiful bound atlases. Traditional cartography makes up the greatest percentage of maps available on the market today, even though digital cartography is a rapidly growing and emerging segment. Traditional maps can be very basic, printed on plain paper with a low retail cost, or may come in a sophisticated, updated, waterproof version carrying a higher retail price. The price of a traditional map is controlled mainly by the quality, accuracy, and uniqueness of the data it is portraying. For example, a road map of U.S. highways is relatively common and does not require incredible accuracy due to its scale, while a sea kayaking map of the Puget Sound is highly specialized and would warrant a higher price.

For geocaching there are a few beneficial types of traditional cartography. First and foremost is a road map of your area. I've been amazed by the number of little parks and side streets in my town that I didn't know existed until I started geocaching. My GPS receiver will certainly help me when I'm out of the car, but getting to and planning how to get to the trailhead has often been aided by a simple printed road map. For those considering traveling farther from home, you may consider a bound road atlas of your state or of North America. Value to expense ratio is very high, with a nicely updated atlas running in the $20 to $30 price range. A recent misconception is that a paper map is not as up-to-date as those found online, but in fact, locally produced maps are often more accurate and up-to-date than many electronic versions. This is especially true if you live in an area with recent growth; online maps may be of little use as their databases are updated far less frequently and on a national level, meaning, sadly, your town might not be the top priority.

In most cases a topographic map will provide you with the best source of terrain information for the area immediately surrounding your geocache. For those of you new to topographic maps, we'll discuss in detail some tips and tricks for reading and interpreting them in Chapter 7. A navigation novice may find using a topo map somewhat intimidating, with its massive amounts of lines and extensive marginalia to decipher. Purchasing a topo map can be a bit of a headache as well.

The United States Geological Survey (USGS) is *the* publisher for seamless nationwide topographic information. Their maps are offered in a variety of sizes and scales, but the most popular and most detailed are the 7.5-minute (minutes of latitude and longitude), 1:24,000 scale series, which are commonly referred to as quads, 7.5-minute maps, or simply, topos. Each map covers an area of approximately fifty square miles and a staggering 55,000-plus titles are available throughout the United States, including Alaska and Hawaii. Unlike most privately produced maps, the coverage of USGS quads is decided upon by their geographic coordinate boundaries with no consideration given to the location of popular geographic features, parks, or urban areas. To illustrate this problem, you simply need to plan one trip with USGS topos. Although fifty square miles sounds like a large area for a map to include, you are more than likely going to find that you'll need two, three, or more topos to cover your whole trip. It is almost a given that the area you are planning on traveling to is near the intersection of at least one other map. For example, Longs Peak, one of the most popular Colorado Fourteeners, lies at the intersection of four USGS topos. If you are an old salt to the outdoors then you know this problem well and certainly have a closet of your house dedicated to old, tattered USGS quad maps.

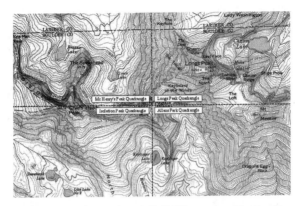

USGS topographic maps are divided by geographic coordinates and do not bend their coverage to accommodate popular areas, as in the example of Longs Peak, Colorado, shown here, where four different quadrangles conjoin. *(Image generated using National Geographic TOPO! State Series, courtesy of National Geographic Maps)*

When setting out to purchase a topo of a particular area, you will certainly be directed to a retailer's USGS selection. Although these maps are the standard for topographic information they are very difficult for retailers to manage as inventory from a cost and profitability standpoint. USGS 7.5-minute maps currently have an MSRP of $6, and for most retailers this is a losing proposition due to the quantity of different titles they must carry in order to at least try to fulfill customers' needs. Before heading in, have a very clear idea of where you are going on your trip and how you plan on getting there. To locate a particular topo you will use a USGS quad index for your state. A quad index provides little detail but shows major roads, cities, and bodies of water, and then overlays a grid of the applicable quad names to each area. Getting your bearings and finding your spot will take a couple of minutes, and then you must hope that the retailer has that one title out of thousands on hand.

Luckily, many private mapping companies have come to the rescue of the outdoor enthusiast by creating updated topographic maps for select, popular recreational areas. Companies such as National Geographic Maps/Trails Illustrated, Tom Harrison, and Green Trails, among many others, have used the base USGS topographic data and then painstakingly updated it to show current trails, roads, campgrounds, and other key information that we're often seeking. These maps are an invaluable tool for a geocacher; they offer the best perspective on the terrain and the most reliable and accurate source of public access. When this is available for the area you are traveling to, the slightly higher retail price is well worth the investment over a USGS 7.5-minute topo. There really is no better bargain when it comes to traditional recreation cartography.

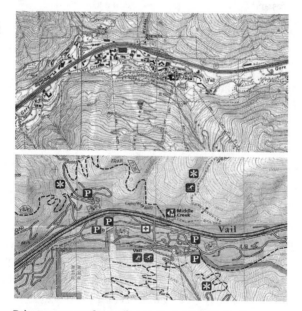

Private cartography, as demonstrated by this Trails Illustrated map, provides more accurate and up-to-date trail and usage information than traditional USGS quads. (*Courtesy of National Geographic Maps*)

Many geocaches are placed off trail, and therefore we should be very considerate about spending as much time on maintained trails as possible, versus bushwhacking and disturbing sensitive environmental areas. USGS topos certainly provide the best topography (in terms of the shape of the Earth), but they are updated far less frequently than private maps. Many public access points, such as trails, roads, campgrounds, etc., are often not displayed, which makes planning an approach to a cache less effective than with a private label's map. In addition, private-label topos are occasionally printed on higher quality materials, such as waterproof, tear-resistant media; are nicely folded; and contain directions for use and other important area information.

The drawback, as you can imagine, is that these companies offer products in limited areas throughout the United States and, in some cases, only publish titles and sell their products regionally. National Geographic Maps/Trails Illustrated has one of the widest selections of recreational maps of the United States, but with a focus on national parks, where geocaching is not allowed. Recently, though, they have expanded their product line and now offer an extensive selection of maps for Colorado and Utah, along with portions of the Southeast, Northeast, and in the very near future, California. Green Trails, based in Washington, has detailed coverage for most of Oregon and Washington, while Tom Harrison has a nice selection of the California Sierra Nevada. While pursuing any type of outdoor activity, including geocaching, you'll find that the cartography produced by the various private-label companies excels far beyond any government, online, or other digital products for accuracy, usefulness, and value.

Digital cartography has really changed the way most people perceive maps. It has become common for many consumers to wonder why purchasing any map is necessary, for the rumor persists that everything is available for free on the Internet. But the truth is you get what you pay for. There are some fantastic map resources on the

Web today, and most of you have probably used them at least once; Mapquest, Rand McNally, Yahoo Maps, and MapBlast are some of the most popular. These Internet sites offer a mix of tools designed to display street maps, driving directions, and atlas-esque maps, in many cases for the world. These online sites can be great for the early stages of planning a geocache hunt. But when the roads get small, turn to dirt, or were very recently installed, you may find yourself in a pinch. With the broad scope of coverage that each company is trying to leverage, maintaining and updating their extensive databases takes time. In my small mountain community I find that driving directions often include "Turn left on Unnamed Road and proceed to Unnamed Road." When searching for topographic maps to get you from the parking lot to the cache, your online options become much more limited. Offroute, National Geographic, Maptech, and even the USGS offer free searchable topographic maps online; however, you are limited to printing a small image of the area, roughly five inches by seven inches, with little to no marginalia, which makes the maps almost impossible to use for navigation. Offroute, National Geographic, and Maptech do offer unique services on their Web sites to design and order custom-printed topos from their databases, which is a spectacular alternative to finding a USGS topo at a retail store. By designing your own coverage you are no longer required to purchase multiple USGS titles. Rather you can opt to have the map printed in a variety of sizes, on a mix of quality medias, and then have the map tubed and shipped to your home for a reasonable price. As you can clearly see, there really isn't a free online topographic option that provides much worth beyond "desk chair" exploring. As for those companies that do offer these databases via the Web, they have realized and are encouraging the value of a printed map.

In addition to Internet-based digital cartography, another popular variation is obtaining topographic maps via software, for example those developed by National Geographic, Maptech, and DeLorme. As a GPS user and geocacher these software programs

Another popular way to obtain topographic maps is via software packages such as those manufactured by National Geographic, DeLorme, and Maptech. *(Photograph by Mike Dyer)*

are invaluable and of great benefit for other outdoor activities as well. All programs offer you a suite of useful tools for planning routes, entering waypoints, and adding personal information such as notes, pictures, Web site links, etc. For geocaching, the greatest advantage is the ability to load select information directly to and from your GPS and print out a custom-designed topo. While these packages are certainly a larger up-front investment than a traditional map or many of the pay-per-use topographic services online, they are far more functional for the purposes of a geocacher and offer a greater value in the long run. If you've spent any time working with your GPS receiver and manually loading the coordinates for a couple caches then you know how long this process can take. Imagine simply drawing a line showing how you want to approach the cache, having the software automatically turn this into a set of waypoints, and then automatically loading this information onto your receiver. What a time-saver! Plus, by having every USGS topo in your state at your fingertips you are saved from the great "topo chase" from store to store or struggling online, enabling you to plan for your next cache hunt with ease. Like many software programs, the differences between the big three map brands come down to functionality, intuitiveness, and data. These packages range in price from $50 to $100, and there are some additional accessory applications available for loading maps onto Palm and Pocket PC OS devices. When choosing an application, I'd recommend a package that uses high quality scans of the official USGS 7.5-minute topographic maps as the base data. There are some packages that offer the entire United States in a single box for $49, which is fantastic value, but the detail you'll want as a geocacher may be lacking.

The final option for getting the exact topo map you need is to use one of the growing numbers of map-on-demand kiosks located at various outdoor retailers nationwide. National Geographic has deployed more than 100 of their MapMachines into these outdoor retailers. The kiosks utilize the same high quality USGS map databases found in their software. This enables you to browse every 7.5-minute topo map in the United States, roughly 55,000 seamless titles, and then center the map on any spot you desire. As an advantage to GPS users like us, you can overlay either a Universal Transverse Mercator (UTM) or latitude and longitude (Lat/Lon) grid on the map, in addition to using the full marginalia of scale bars, magnetic declination, and corner coordinates found on the original USGS maps. Once you've centered your cache, overlaid grids, and selected any of the kiosk's other features, maps take about

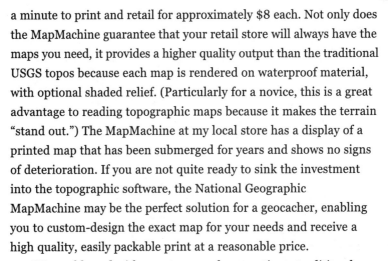

a minute to print and retail for approximately $8 each. Not only does the MapMachine guarantee that your retail store will always have the maps you need, it provides a higher quality output than the traditional USGS topos because each map is rendered on waterproof material, with optional shaded relief. (Particularly for a novice, this is a great advantage to reading topographic maps because it makes the terrain "stand out.") The MapMachine at my local store has a display of a printed map that has been submerged for years and shows no signs of deterioration. If you are not quite ready to sink the investment into the topographic software, the National Geographic MapMachine may be the perfect solution for a geocacher, enabling you to custom-design the exact map for your needs and receive a high quality, easily packable print at a reasonable price.

We are blessed with a vast array of map options: traditional, digital, Internet, software, and on-demand kiosks. Having a high quality map with you in the field is essential from a safety stand-point and also a wise tool for enhancing your probability of finding the cache. As a planning resource, a variety of maps—road and topographic—are an essential time-saver and strategy enhancer from both a cache finding and hiding standpoint. In the checklist section in the back of this book you'll find a simplified cheat sheet to the tools of the trade. Before investing any money, grab the cheat sheet, visit some of the Web sites of the listed companies, and head to your local specialty retailer.

Although we've certainly covered a long list of equipment, remember, to get started you need only a few essentials: a GPS unit, a map of your area, coordinates to your cache, and, wisely, a compass. As your dedication to the sport grows or as you become increasingly involved in other outdoor activities, you can always supplement your gear closet with software, fully featured GPS units, and the other goodies we've discussed.

# Chapter 3
## Outdoor Ethics and Wilderness Safety

## General Wilderness Safety Principles

Geocaches are often placed in unique locations. Some might never require that you leave the safety of your car, while others might require technical climbing skills or even spelunking. Any type of outdoor activity involves consideration of the safety precautions you should take prior to heading out the door. It is up to you to weigh the complexity of your excursions as part of the planning process and make a concerted effort at taking precautions in order to keep yourself safe and your geocaching experience fun.

The first and foremost step to a safe trip outdoors is notification. For any outdoor activity that may take you to an unknown location it's common sense to notify people regarding when you are leaving, where you are going, and how long you anticipate being out. As a technically inclined group, geocachers also have the unique ability to provide coordinates of their planned destination, and, in many cases, where they'll be starting. Nearly all search and rescue groups in the country are outfitted with GPS units, and providing coordinates of your trip will certainly aid in finding you if something goes wrong.

The next step to having a safe trip is to wear appropriate clothing. In many cases, having the correct technical clothing can make the difference between having either a fun and safe trip or a miserable and dangerous one. There is nothing worse than being freezing cold or wet, or even unnecessarily hot, on an outdoor trip. Dressing in layers is by far the best advice that anyone can provide. It is also important to wear the correct type of clothing for the conditions. We've heard that "cotton kills," but neither synthetic fabrics nor cotton will keep you warm if you don't have an adequate shell to keep moisture and wind off your body. Listen to weather reports and respect the elements, especially in places such as mountain ranges, narrow canyons, and exposed areas. During the summer here in the Rockies, I can set my watch by the afternoon thunderstorms. Therefore a cache hunt in high elevation needs to take into account the often radically shifting weather conditions, both in terms of when to start the day and what clothing to pack.

Another component of safety is having the appropriate equipment for your task. Every equipment list should contain a well-outfitted first-aid kit. Several companies make prebuilt kits designed specifically for the types of common injuries suffered in the field. These kits range in complexity from basic to advanced and are typically based on the number of people utilizing the supplies as well as the type of activity. For most day hikes a simple kit including Band-Aids, tape, wraps, pain reliever, blister repair, and bite kits is all that is necessary. Many quality outdoor retailers have a preparedness section in their stores, complete with individual supplies along with the prebuilt kits mentioned above.

Equipment also refers to everything you have on or carry with you when you leave your car. This includes appropriate footwear, technical outerwear, a GPS unit, compass, maps, and any specialty equipment such as climbing and spelunking gear. I am not an expert climber nor a spelunker, and therefore will not attempt to describe the right equipment for those activities. But in general it is important that all equipment you take into the outdoors be in good repair and appropriate for the elements and constraints of your trip. I have a tendency to overprepare for even the shortest of trips and have constructed an emergency supply kit, along with my first-aid kit, that I carry when on the trail. This kit contains waterproof matches, a signaling mirror, pocketknife, long-burning candle, small roll of duct tape, parachute cord, Velcro pieces, and a spare cam lock buckle or two. Even on a day hike, when I never *plan* to be out overnight, I prepare to be *stuck* overnight in the unlikely instance that someone gets too hurt to hike out or that dangerous weather pins me down. A few simple items such as waterproof matches and a candle can make the difference between cold and wet versus warm and dry. And a backup cam lock buckle can keep a backpack on your back instead of clutched in your arms. Perhaps it is the Eagle Scout in me or fear of Murphy's Law; I have yet to use any of these backup items over years of trips, but knowing they are there in case I need them is reassuring.

Food and hydration are other critical elements of your equipment. Hydration packs really work well to solve the challenge of carrying water or an energy drink, and many units double as backpacks, perfect for carrying additional gear. The rule of thumb is to drink a liter of cool, clean water per hour of moderate to strenuous activity. The human body cannot absorb much more than that, and since water is heavy deadweight in your pack, do not unnecessarily carry too much. Estimate how long you plan to be out and carry an appropriate amount of water for that time period. If you are incorporating a geocache event into a longer multiday trip you may consider investing in a water filter or other purification device versus carrying an extreme amount of water. Hydration equipment has become a multimillion dollar business; it has been scientifically proven that correct hydration yields better human performance.

As for food, a lot of this depends on your personal tastes and metabolism. There are a wide variety of energy bars in various flavors and consistencies, but standbys such as GORP, trail mixes, granola bars, and fruit are also excellent items for an on-trail snack. Make sure you are taking along enough food to keep your energy up and stay motivated in order to complete your goals but are not overdoing it. Caching is a great family activity, so in many cases you may consider a more substantial picnic lunch as part of your afternoon.

Overall, having a fun and safe day of geocaching is the goal. The simplest way to ensure this is preparation. You do not need to spend a lot of money on technical equipment or on an expedition-quality first-aid kit to have a safe adventure, but be sure to weigh the risks and take the appropriate precautions. If outdoor safety and first aid interest you more, I'd encourage either taking a class from your local hiking club or picking up a book dedicated to the subject. The techniques you'll learn will be valuable as a geocacher and for any other physical activity you are involved in.

## Outdoor Ethics

Geocaching will introduce you to some beautiful and remote public lands, parks, and wilderness areas, many of which you've not yet been to but you may certainly come back to after experiencing them first-hand. The challenge we are beginning to face is the numbers of people seeking the same cache, one you may have just found, along with the numbers of people participating in other outdoor activities in the same area. Geocaching is introducing a new group of people to the outdoors, and in some cases, to unimproved areas where each person may have his or her own interpretation of how best to get there. A popular cache may be visited more than fifty times a year, and the possibility of damage to the environment around the cache grows with human activity and pressure.

Therefore, we must take the lead on preserving the lands we visit and ensure that we have the least possible impact while enjoying our sport. There are many nonprofit organizations that have crafted outdoor ethics and principles we should follow. The principles of Leave No Trace (LNT) are the most recognized guidelines for appropriate use of the outdoors and are listed on the following pages. It is important to consider these principles both while hunting for a stash or considering placement of a new one.

## Plan Ahead and Prepare
- Know the regulations and special concerns for the area you'll visit.
- Prepare for extreme weather, hazards, and emergencies.
- Schedule your trip to avoid times of high use.
- Visit in small groups. Split larger parties into groups of four to six.
- Use a map and compass to eliminate the use of marking paint, rock cairns, or flagging.
- Repackage food to minimize waste.

## Travel and Camp on Durable Surfaces
- Durable surfaces include established trails and campsites, rock, gravel, dry grasses, or snow.
- Protect riparian areas by camping at least 200 feet from lakes and streams.
- Good campsites are found, not made. Altering a site is not necessary.

**In popular areas:**
- Concentrate use on existing trails and campsites.
- Walk single file in the middle of the trail, even when wet or muddy.
- Keep campsites small. Focus activity on areas where vegetation is absent.

**In pristine areas:**
- Disperse use to prevent the creation of campsites and trails.
- Avoid places where impacts are just beginning.

## Dispose of Waste Properly
- Pack it in, pack it out. Inspect your campsite and rest areas for trash or spilled foods. Pack out all trash, leftover food, and litter.
- Deposit solid human waste in cat holes dug six to eight inches deep at least 2,000 feet from water, camp, and trails. Cover and disguise your cat hole when finished.
- Pack out toilet paper and hygiene products.
- To wash yourself or your dishes, carry water 200 feet away from streams or lakes and use small amounts of biodegradable soap. Scatter strained dishwater.

## Leave What You Find
- Preserve the past; examine, but do not touch, cultural or historic structures and artifacts.
- Leave rocks, plants, and other natural objects as you find them.
- Avoid introducing or transporting nonnative species.
- Do not build structures, furniture, or dig trenches.

## Minimize Campfire Impacts
- Campfires can cause lasting impacts to the backcountry. Use a lightweight stove for cooking and enjoy a candle lantern for light.
- Where fires are permitted, use established fire rings, fire pans, or mound fires.
- Keep fires small. Only use sticks from the ground that can be broken by hand.
- Burn all wood and coals to ash, put out fires completely, and then scatter cool ashes.

**Respect Wildlife**
- Observe wildlife from a distance. Do not follow or approach them.
- Never feed animals. Feeding wildlife damages their health, alters natural behaviors, and exposes them to predators and other dangers.
- Control pets at all times or leave them at home.
- Avoid wildlife during sensitive times: mating, nesting, raising young, or winter.

**Be Considerate of Other Visitors**
- Respect other visitors and protect the quality of their experience.
- Be courteous. Yield to other users on the trail.
- Step to the downhill side of the trail when encountering pack stock.
- Take breaks and camp away from trails and other visitors.
- Let nature's sounds prevail. Avoid loud voices and noises.

This copyrighted information has been reprinted with permission from the Leave No Trace Center for Outdoor Ethics. For more information or materials, please visit www.LNT.org or call 1-800-332-4100.

In addition to following the principles of Leave No Trace, Geocaching.com is encouraging Cache In Trash Out (CITO) events as a way for geocachers to organize land stewardship activities. It's always a great idea, and socially conscious, to bring along a plastic grocery bag and fill it up with garbage on your hike out. It's amazing how much litter abounds in our parks and manages to blow off the trail into seemingly pristine areas. Take a moment to make the place better for the next cacher.

When considering our impact on pristine environments, also take into account your own movements as they can sometimes remove the disguise of a well hidden cache. For example, a cache I found recently was neatly tucked into a rock outcropping and nearly invisible from all angles, yet the base of the rock outcropping showed heavily disturbed pine needles, loose soil, and footprints. This was a dead giveaway to the cache location. Be careful not to disturb the area surrounding your hunted cache, both from an eco-logical and game playing standpoint. After placing the cache back in its location, look around and cover your tracks if possible. This is a great game courtesy that I wish more people took the time to do.

# Chapter 4
## Basic Geocaching Principles

Getting started in geocaching is simple and fun, and I hope that by this point in the book you haven't been too terribly turned off by the jargon, equipment, outdoor safety concerns, and other technicalities necessary to continue your pursuit. With some building blocks now behind us we can march forward and take an in-depth look at geocaching, starting with the very basics of the game and then delving into a how-to approach.

## What Is in a Cache?

Caching began long before GPS receivers became popular, and in fact, long before the United States even took shape. Fur trappers, explorers, and indigenous peoples placed caches loaded with food, furs, and other supplies in hidden locations in order to sustain their travels and alleviate the necessity of carrying all the needed provisions. Even today, through hikers on the Pacific Crest Trail, Continental Divide Trail, and Appalachian Trail will often plan months in advance of beginning their treks by placing caches of food, water, and critical supplies such as fresh shoelaces, boots, and socks in strategic locations along the route. In geocaching the items contained in the boxes are certainly not necessities; they are more often than not a mix of eclectic junk, for lack of a better term. Certainly, the thrill and enjoyment in geocaching comes from the "thrill of the hunt" rather than the value of the trinkets you collect along the way.* I joke that geocaching has enabled me to rid the drawers in my house of silly items I've picked up at trade shows, in cereal boxes, and from flea markets. From the look of the caches I've located, it seems I'm not alone.

*Note: There are a few types of cache games that do not have cache boxes, as is the case in virtual, webcam, locationless, and event caches.

The only requirement for a geocaching cache box is a logbook. A pen or pencil is usually included in a cache box too, yet micro-caches may not have enough room for a writing implement, so it is a good practice to carry one with you just in case. Most cache creators include a letter notifying nongeocachers of what they've found and what to do in case they locate the cache by accident. In addition to the required log, pen, and perhaps a notification letter, cache items for trade generally include small trinkets such as marbles, key chains, coins, and other gadgets. One way people introduce unique-ness to their particular cache is by requiring items of a certain genre to be traded. For example, if the creator indicates that this is a buffalo-related cache, then all items contained must relate to that animal. Other spins on this are "libraries," in which only paperback books are exchanged, or audio and video tapes.

A typical geocache. *(Photograph by Mike Dyer)*

Geocachers participate in many hobbies, and it shows through the wide range of cache items in the field. I prefer to leave something useful at each cache, usually a map of the area, but anything will suffice as long as it fits inside the box. If you have the means to leave a great reward behind for a fellow cacher, certainly do so, for no one will object. When creating your own cache, you may wish to reward the first finder with a few great prize options, especially if the cache takes some significant skill or gumption to locate.

In addition to the mix of trinkets, there are a few extraordinary items you may stumble upon, specifically Travel Bugs, Geocoins, and other traveling, trackable items. Best described as traveling trinkets,

The Son of Frankenstein Travel Bug.
*(Photograph by Mike Dyer)*

these and other similar variations are destined to move from cache to cache while their whereabouts are tracked via the Web. A Travel Bug, for example, is a dog tag–like device with a unique serial number engraved upon it. The tag is attached to an item, placed in a cache, given a name, and then those who find and move it update its whereabouts. Some Travel Bugs have crossed oceans, visited hundreds of cache sites, and are still in the field traveling today. Bugs may have a specific destination that they are trying to reach or a goal, such as to "travel to three continents." If you find a Travel Bug or any other type of serial-numbered trinket, simply go to the Web site listed on the item and follow any specific instructions. Usually it is as simple as logging where you found the item, that you took it, and what cache you placed the item in thereafter.

Disposable cameras are also popular cache contents. If there is film left, snap a picture of yourself and fellow geocachers on the trail. If you happen to take the last picture it is good etiquette to notify the cache owner that the camera is spent and ready for developing. Some cache owners will later post the pictures on the Web, so check back to see how yours turned out. As a secondary means of documentation, I like to take a digital picture of all the caches I've located. Photos are a great way to remember all of your finds and may provide some fodder for a good cache design or hiding spot idea for the future.

There are a few things you should never find in a cache. You should never encounter anything illicit, meaning drugs, alcohol, or anything considered a weapon or dangerous. If you do, it is wise to notify the cache owner via e-mail that his or her cache has been tampered with. Another item that is not smart for caches is food. Remember that geocaches are outdoors and wildlife have an incredible way of finding anything edible or anything that may even smell edible, such as scented stickers or dental floss, for example. Animals will likely tear, chew, and destroy any cache with food items in it. If you wish to leave something refreshing for a fellow cacher, choose something innocuous such as bottled water, but bear in mind that it may freeze and break its package and then flood the cache with water when it thaws. So the best advice I have is to leave the food and water in your pack, not the cache.

## Game Types and Cache Sizes

Geocaching is a rapidly evolving sport. Just four years ago, when the first few caches were hidden, the premise of the game was simple: using your GPS, find a small package that someone else had hidden in an obscure place. Today cachers are becoming more adventurous and sophisticated with their cache designs, and certainly by the time this book is printed and in your hands other new geocache games and clever variations will have been devised. Since geocaching is such a new sport, most people do not know that there are, in fact, a wide variety of geocaching games. Just like you can play full-court, half-court, HORSE, and Around the World with a basketball, the original geocache game has spawned a mix of spin-offs. The genesis of these new games has resulted in the creation of standards to make it easy for a geocacher to see what they're getting into. There are currently two main categories used to define all geocaches: game type and relative cache size.

Regular caches, sometimes called original or traditional cache games, are the bread and butter of the sport and make up the greatest percentage of all hidden caches. The traditional cache game is the least complex, easiest to learn and master, and makes up a part of all other cache games. The concept behind a traditional cache is for one geocacher to create and hide a cache in a public space for some-one else to find with the geographic coordinates provided to its hiding spot using a GPS receiver. Traditional caches can be any of three sizes, which will be discussed in detail later. These and all other caches must meet the basic rules of placement, meaning that the cache must be in a publicly accessible location and not in a national park, wildlife preserve, military installation, or on any other protected land. Traditional cache games rely mainly on your technique for searching an area, rather than your problem-solving or navigational skills, which are emphasized in other game types. However, this doesn't mean that finding a traditional cache will be easy, nor will it be any less fun and intriguing than other games. While traditional caches may lack the complexity of other types, their abundance and ease of creation means that you will end up traveling to lots of new places and will be looking at the world around you in a different way. After finding a few traditional caches in my neighborhood, I began visualizing great hiding places for caches of my own. I've had some wild and wacky experiences with traditional caches and have ended up exploring parks and trail systems that I didn't know existed. Keep in mind that the basic concept of finding a cache that someone else has hidden permeates through all cache games, just like shooting a basketball at the hoop is an essential ingredient in all variations of basketball. As a new geocacher you will complete more traditional cache games than any other type.

Once you understand the traditional game it is easy to imagine how the idea for the next game was spawned; it is a logical step up in complexity, requiring the seeker to locate more than one cache to complete the game.

A multicache, rightfully named because it has more than one hidden cache box, requires the seeker to locate several caches in sequence in order to find the final box. Best likened to playing hopscotch, completing a multicache requires jumping from cache to cache and learning coordinates that will eventually lead you to the final box and potentially treasures. Multicache games can require any number of steps, but the simplest form requires just finding the first cache, which contains coordinates to the second and final cache boxes.

One of the more popular spins on the multicache game incorporates several small caches that include portions of the coordinate for the final cache. While the final cache box can be of any accepted size, it is typical that the subcaches are small and only contain a piece of paper. For this reason, 35-mm film canisters or other tiny plastic containers are most common for the subcaches. When reviewing a list of caches in your area you'll see multicaches denoted with an icon of two boxes with yellow lids, as opposed to the singular green-lidded box of a traditional cache. Multicaches are more challenging than traditional cache games but only in regard to the skill of seeking; typically, they do not require any special problem-solving skills as other variations might.

Blurring the lines between a multicache and a puzzle cache, to be discussed later, is a variation in which each step may require deciphering a riddle to reveal directions to the next cache location. One of my favorite local caches is a multicache located in a large open field. At the start of the game you are provided coordinates to three distinct microcaches. Inside each microcache is a bearing from its location to the final cache box. To complete the game successfully you must locate the three microcaches, retrieve the bearings they include, and then perform triangulation with a compass in order to find the final cache. This particular variation truly exemplifies all the aspects of geocaching, with a great test of your GPS, cache finding, and navigational skills rolled into one fun package. This multicache is far more involved than most and should probably be designated as a puzzle cache, but since it involves finding more than one cache to complete it falls into the category of a multicache game.

By adding a slight twist to a multicache game you arrive at an offset cache. Similar to the multicache, an offset requires the cache seeker to find more than one location. But instead of finding multiple cache boxes, the first location found in an offset cache is typically a plaque, sign, or memorial whose contents solve a riddle, a puzzle, or complete a phrase that leads you to the final cache box. Seekers are provided the coordinates to the starting location and the puzzle that they must solve or decipher. The deciphered directions may come in the form of another coordinate or a bearing from your current location and the distance to the next cache. Therefore, offset caches will often test your ability to solve riddles and, in some instances, your navigational skills beyond the basic aspects of using a GPS receiver. Offset caches share the same icon on Geocaching.com as multi-caches: a pair of boxes with yellow lids. With offset caches a distance of roughly two miles from the starting point to the final cache box is typical, so you may end up needing to get back in the car and travel across town or to a different park, but certainly not to another county. Another twist may require that you locate several cache boxes, similar to a multicache game. While an offset cache does introduce a puzzle or clue that needs to be solved, they are usually less complicated then the next form of the game, a puzzle cache.

Puzzle caches, occasionally referred to as mystery caches, can require the most complex problem solving compared to any other type of geocache game. Puzzles can be of nearly any type and form, ranging from math and logic problems to answering local history questions. Puzzle caches start by providing you with a coordinate that is *not* to the final cache location, as well as a puzzle that you will need to solve once you've arrived there. From your surroundings you will be able to complete the puzzle and learn the resting place of the final cache. As with offset caches, the geocache Web site requests that the final location be no farther than two miles from the starting point, for the sake of maintaining accurate distance calculations on items such as Travel Bugs and for general accessibility.

Puzzle cache types can be a bit of a "catchall," to paraphrase the Geocaching.com Web site, because a wide range of variations and types of geocache games fall under this category. A local puzzle cache in my town leads you to the parking lot of the public library; after solving a simple riddle, you learn your fate is to enter the library and search for a logbook that is hidden among GPS books in a travel section. More complicated versions I've seen online have required estimating distances, trigonometry functions, and some very advanced map reading and orienteering skills. But others seem rather easy, requiring only that you do a little *post facto* homework. An example would be to arrive at a park and locate a rock wall with Native paintings. In order to solve the puzzle, you must learn which tribe created what you are seeing and what the painting represents. Your answers to the puzzle are e-mailed to the cache creator as verification that you found the correct location and accurately completed the puzzle. While a logbook is considered the minimum requirement for a cache to be considered "legal," in this scenario, and in some other geocaching variations, you may find that neither a physical cache box nor a physical logbook exists.

Beyond the traditional, multi-, offset, and puzzle cache games the types of geocaches change radically into four distinct "hide-and-go-seek" games, far different from the regular cache game.

The first type, letterboxing, is a unique game similar to geo-caching in which people search for a hidden box that contains a logbook and a specific rubber stamp. Letterbox seekers use a set of clues, sometimes cryptic, which may or may not require navigational skills to locate the box. Once the box is found, the seekers stamp the logbook with their own stamps and in turn stamp their personal log-books with the stamp from the letterbox. Letterboxing has been around for longer than geocaching, originating in England. It began to grow here in the United States in the late '80s and early '90s. While not as popular as geocaching, there are a growing number of letterboxes nationwide. Currently, there are approximately 8,500.

Since the original letterboxing game did not require the use of geographic coordinates as clues, nor a GPS for that matter, geocachers and letterboxers have come together to create an integrated version of the game known as a letterbox hybrid. A letterbox hybrid cache game is nearly identical to the traditional geocache game in form, yet the box must contain the basics of letterboxing: a rubber stamp and logbook. In some instances letterboxes have items for trade, but it is not a required part of the game. As you find more traditional geocaches you will probably find pages in logbooks marked with a rubber stamp, which are often the marks of a letterboxer who has found this cache. Since the two games are so similar in their design, letterboxing and geocaching certainly share a lot of the same participants. Letterbox hybrids are indicated by envelope icon on the Geocaching.com Web site. But to learn more about and participate in the original letterboxing game visit www.letterboxing.org, which appears to be the equivalent of Geocaching.com for this sport.

For cache seekers who like to see themselves on TV, a webcam cache is an odd twist on geocaching that will satisfy your desire for two seconds of fame. If you haven't already noticed, there are an increasing number of webcams everywhere. Whether they are at intersections, freeways, and city centers, or in large public gathering places such as sports complexes or clubs, you can barely escape the ever-watchful eye of the camera. If you do a "google" or other Internet search for "Denver webcam," you will return dozens of page links to Web sites with live pictures. Opening one of these pages reveals a live shot from that particular camera and, in some cases, the ability to review previous hours or days of pictures. A webcam cache does not have a physical cache box or logbook, but instead requires having your picture taken by the webcam and then going online and retrieving the captured image of yourself. The cache creators then require that you e-mail your picture to them as proof of finding the camera. In some instances they may even ask that you do something funny or hold your GPS in plain view as further proof that you located the camera with your GPS receiver. Webcam caches include the coordinate you need to navigate to, any particular things you must include in your picture, and a link to the Web page you later retrieve your picture from. As you might expect, the icon on Geocaching.com is, of course, a webcam.

Next on the list of game types is a virtual cache, which is tailored to those who would like to visit someplace "magical" or unique. "Virtual," in this case, means that there isn't a physical cache to find but instead you are provided coordinates to a particular location, which has unbelievable natural beauty, uniqueness, or ambiance. To verify that you have found the desired location you must report what you found, and often what you saw or experienced, to the cache inventor. Since geocaches and geocaching are not allowed in national parks, preserves, or monuments, virtual caches may sidestep the rules by not placing anything at these protected sites but directing people to an already prepared viewing location. For example, a virtual cache may take you to the statue of Stonewall Jackson at the Bull Run Battlefield in Virginia or to the observation deck and plaque at the Old Faithful geyser. Closer to home, a virtual cache may lead you to something as simple as a downtown wall covered with street art from a famous artist or to the top floor of a huge building for sweeping downtown views. Wherever the location, the object of the game is that you will see and experience what the cache creator deems truly incredible to see.

An even stranger spin on a virtual cache requires no movement at all, except for your mouse and fingers across the keys as you navigate a series of Web pages to a specific location. Although it certainly defeats the fun and purpose of geocaching, this spin on the game has become a marketing tool for some companies, bouncing the Internet surfer from custom page to custom page. The final Web address holds a prize that is only revealed after completing the Web site tour in sequence.

Yet another type of geocaching game is an event cache. In this case, it's an event for geocachers to discuss geocaching. Creating a cache event is a great way to pull like-minded individuals together to learn about each others' strategies and plans for creating new caches, and it can serve as a terrific means of starting a local geocache club. The coordinates provided to the event are the "directions" to the party and include information such as date, time to arrive, and what to bring. Event caches posted on the Internet are specifically for the purpose of furthering geocaching, and guidelines state that the event cannot be for a group geocache hunt or getting people to a nongeocaching event—no matter how great the concert or tempting it may be to assemble a mountain bike ride among friends. However, if you do participate in a local geocache club the rules for planning events of this type may be different inside your circle. An event cache is the only geocaching game that has a predetermined life expectancy, which terminates on the date and time of the event.

Different, but of the same motivation, are Cache In Trash Out (CITO) events, in which a specific date, time, and location are selected for geocachers to come together and take part in improving the environment. This can include packing out litter and other trash left behind by less conscientious people or providing helping hands for trail maintenance, seedling plantings, or other land stewardship. In 2003 geocachers participated in more than sixty unique CITO events, and there is encouragement to do more every year. Those interested in organizing a CITO should begin by contacting their local parks and recreation department or a volunteer agency such as Volunteers for Outdoor Colorado, Fourteeners Initiative, Pacific Crest Trail Association, or others. From these groups find out what can be done to assist in land stewardship activities. Then it's just a matter of posting the event on Geocaching.com

The final unique geocaching games are reverse caches, otherwise known as locationless caches. Unlike every other cache game where you are provided with a coordinate in order to navigate to and find something, a reverse cache provides a specific item to find in the world, and to succeed you must provide coordinates to those items you've located. Locationless caches are very similar to scavenger hunts rather than the hide-and-go-seek concept of the traditional games. A locationless cache may require finding campgrounds, tennis courts, UPS drop boxes, or the highest points in your county, for example. Once you find one of the specified items and record its coordinate you post it to the cache's Web site. As other seekers of the same locationless cache find additional examples a list is generated of all the points in which you can locate the specified item. The caches may be goofy and rather pointless but fun, or they may generate a list of locations that are useful. But remember, this version of the game does not include a physical cache box or logbook, making it entirely different from the traditional geocache game. On Geocaching.com a locationless cache icon appears as Earth with a flag stuck atop it. To participate in a locationless cache game you will need to navigate your way to the page specifically for this cache type because it will not appear if you do a normal search for nearby caches.

Many cache games can blur the lines between multiple game types. For example, you can participate in a multivirtual cache, where you go from one site to another, collecting nothing and signing no logs while being led along by your geocache tour director to points of extraordinary interest. Within a few miles from my house I've been fortunate to find a mix of unique caches ranging from logbooks hidden in libraries to microcaches hidden in a busy parking lot to a large cache containing bunches of little caches, appropriately named "seed pod."

Variation and improvisation are what make geocaching so dynamic and captivating for participants. No two cache games are alike. Even basic caches are all hidden in unique locations. But with the creative spin that many cache creators have added to their particular games, geocaches truly have infinite variety.

The newest relative to geocaching is benchmark hunting. A benchmark is a permanently affixed mark, symbol, or brass plaque which has a precise elevation above sea level and a geographic coordinate. Benchmarks are everywhere across the country; you have probably walked past a couple of them strolling through town and never noticed. Most commonly, a benchmark is not an obvious plaque but instead an engraved mark, which looks like a spirit level (a sight with a tripod base) etched into a stone, concrete walk, or a wall. Similar to finding a virtual cache, you are given the coordinates of the benchmark and set out to find it without discovering a physical cache or signing a log. Dissimilar to all other caches, there are instances in which only a set of verbal directions, versus a geographic coordinator, are provided to locate the benchmark. These directions may include specific distances and bearings from permanent landmarks or simple descriptions of placement, for example: "Benchmark located on the NE corner on the cornerstone of the First Methodist Church in downtown Denver, CO." Many benchmarks are located on private property, in government facilities, or in other restricted areas, so be sure to check a map and do not cross any "No Trespassing" signs—no matter how tempting and close the caches may be. A benchmark may be buried under dirt, leaves, or other sediment materials, so, unlike in normal geocaching, you may need to do some scratching around to find it. When you do, dust it off, make a note of its condition, and perhaps take a picture. Whatever you do, do not remove or deface benchmarks; they are cool and would certainly make a great souvenir but they are an important part of our national history and are used by surveyors to this day. Like any ordinary cache, the final step is logging your find, and in this case also the benchmark's condition, on the Web site.

At the start of this chapter I noted there are two unique ways to identify all cache games. First was the game type. The second characteristic is size of the physical cache. Keep in mind that some geocaching games do not have a physical cache and therefore would not include this category. But since the bulk of all caches in the field are traditional games, this distinction can be very important.

The sizes of geocaches fall into three categories: micro, regular, and large. A microcache has a box approximately the size of a 35-mm film canister, matchbox, or small mint tin. Regular caches, the most common of the three sizes found in the field today, are usually plastic containers or ammo boxes, roughly eight inches tall by eight inches wide, or a few pints in total volume. Large caches can be as immense as five-gallon plastic buckets or large plastic tubs, such as those commonly seen at discount stores around the holidays and used for storing wrapping papers and such. Cache size plays an important role in the game, from both a finding and hiding strategy standpoint. Obviously, a large cache will need to be hidden in a less discrete location than a 35-mm film canister. Since caches cannot be buried or require tools to find, a large cache must be placed in, under, or around a natural feature with enough mass to obstruct it from view from the general public. Be sure to make note of the descriptions of all caches included in a game. As you've learned, many game types include multiple cache boxes, and usually the size of the cache is only shown for the final cache box. Reading the creator's detailed game description will usually provide the size, color, and any other defining characteristics he or she feels are necessary to correctly identify the cache(s) in the field.

Due to its durability, an ammo box is one of the most common regular cache containers. *(Photograph by Mike Dyer)*

## Rules and General Guidelines

As in any game, there are, of course, some rules to geocaching, and in this sport the guidelines pertain mainly to hiding and creating your own caches rather than specific rules for finding them. Geocaching.com has an extensive set of guidelines that detail the requirements they use for posting a new cache, thus making it "legal." If you plan on using their site as the core for your geocaching experience it is best to begin by carefully reading and understanding their guidelines. The same suggestion is recommended if you belong to a local geocache club. Be sure to collect the club's guidelines in addition to following the simplified set of general rules I've written here.

Geocaching is meant to be a fun and safe sport for all ages. Therefore, the first rule of thumb when creating a cache is to ensure it is safe for others to find. Caches should not be located near active railroad tracks, on the side of busy roads, or in a location where suspicious activity may cause alarm, for example on the outskirts of an airport, at a dam, or in urban transportation hubs, especially in these days of heightened concern over terrorism.

There are specific types of managed land where geocaching is strictly prohibited. National Park Service property or lands managed by the U.S. Fish and Wildlife Service, which are usually wildlife protection and management areas, are considered out of bounds for geocaching. In some cases you may be able to post virtual caches in these areas, but be certain that the cache can be reached without leaving maintained trails and roads. Military installations, archeological and historic sites, and other places sensitive to human impact are also off-limits to geocaching. Caches should only be hidden in areas that are accessible to the general public and do not jeopardize the environment, cross any private property, or break covenants of the area. While most U.S. Forest Service, Bureau of Land Management (BLM), state, county, and city parks allow geocaching, research any specific rules they may have before hiding or seeking a cache.

As a geocache creator you are solely responsible for maintaining your cache. This includes its Web site, physical location, condition, and impact it may have. Hiding a cache that you cannot easily maintain and reach is unacceptable. You are required to review the logs pertaining to your cache and react to notes regarding bad coordinates, damage done to the cache, or concerns that your visitors have posted. Occasional checkups are a great idea, to make sure that foot traffic is not damaging the land around your cache and that critical items such as your logbook and pen are still functional. If for some reason your cache has been poached or should not be visited, make it inactive to hunting until you fix the problem.

Caches should not be buried or placed inside an urban container, such as a light post electrical box, that will necessitate the seeker to use any tools whatsoever. Good hiding spots range from hollows in stumps and downed trees to cracks in boulders. Covering your cache with nearby rocks or dead branches is acceptable, but remember to keep impact slim to none. If your hiding spot requires a lot of "add-ons" to be effective then you may want to reconsider the location and continue your search for that *perfect* location.

As geocaching has grown in popularity it has begun to develop some growing pains. A friend of mine was hiking with a group of people on BLM land in Utah and was stopped by an angry park ranger wondering if they were geocaching. It seems there are several caches located in areas in the park where foot traffic was causing severe erosion and now the park is cracking down. To protect the future of this sport and maintain its growth, we need to respect the guidelines set forth and protect the lands and places we use.

When geocaching, if for any reason you feel that your actions may cause alarm or if you are aware of damage or other concerns that could arise from your activities while participating in the sport, stop. Geocaching is meant to be a fun and relaxing way to enjoy the outdoors and GPS technology. Keeping the game safe equals fun for all.

# Chapter 5
## Finding Your First Cache

Finding a geocache is as much about your GPS skills as it is about your searching aptitude. Your navigational skills will lead you so close to the cache that you can smell it, but not quite close enough to see it. The final thirty feet of any cache game is the most difficult and the most exhilarating part. As you successfully complete more caches you will learn a few tricks of the trade, and you will certainly develop your own system for locating those especially well-hidden boxes. Plus, you are likely to pick up on some common ways in which caches are concealed. Navigational skills are the essential ingredient for geocaching, and if you're not yet comfortable with your GPS, map, and compass, with a couple of hints and some practice you will be by the end of this book.

Your first foray into finding a geocache is receiving the key details about a particular cache. This can be as simple as creating an account on Geocaching.com, the sport's main worldwide Web site, or joining a local club or group. Getting started on the Internet is very simple and requires creating a user name and account, similar to signing up for any newsletter or other Internet-based group. Once logged in, it's time to choose your first cache to find, and nothing could be simpler.

Using the search tools provided, simply enter the coordinate of your house or your zip code, and a list of geocaches in your area will be provided, sorted by distance. If there are a lot of caches in your area you can narrow the options by using an advanced search tool, limiting caches to within a certain mile radius, area code, or keyword. Geocaching.com labels each cache with a relative difficulty and terrain rating system of one to five stars, more stars being more difficult. The number of stars for both search difficulty and terrain are supplied by the cache creator, after using a step-by-step tool for determination. The system seems to work pretty well but, quite often, I find that most caches fall into the obscure medium range.

A screen shot, courtesy of Geocaching.com, showing a typical list of caches after a zip code search.

For your first cache select one that is relatively easy to find, and if you are new to hiking and the outdoors select an easy to moderate terrain as well. Between the two the terrain difficulty is the one you'll want to pay close attention to, making sure it meets your stamina and physical abilities. In addition to the rating system, Geocaching.com places icons next to each cache to denote what type of cache game it is. A single green box is a regular or traditional cache; two yellow boxes is a multi- or offset cache; a ghost is a virtual cache; a question mark is a mystery cache; an envelope is a letterbox cache; a text balloon is an event cache; a camera is a webcam cache; and the Earth with a flag stuck in it is a locationless cache. Those seeking Travel Bugs will see Travel Bug icons next to the game icons during times when one is at that particular cache. The Travel Bugs appear as dog tag–shaped items with spiderlike icons. You can certainly do a multi-, offset, or virtual cache for your first find, but to begin I think you'll learn a lot from the simple experience of finding a traditional cache.

Once you have narrowed down some options in your area, open

each cache, read its description, and verify that it's something you are up for. There is a cache in my town, for example, that requires ten miles of hiking round-trip, and another one that requires some minor caving. The cache page on the Internet will notify the seeker of any special equipment they may need to bring, i.e., a flashlight for peering into dark spaces, calculator for solving a riddle, pen to sign the log, etc. The cache page will also tell you what to expect for the hike to the cache and details on where to park or any necessary park entrance fees.

Once you've picked your desired game, either write down its coordinate or download it to your computer for automatic loading to a GPS. (It is important to note that you will need software that can read either the .gpx or .loc file type if you want to automatically transfer the information to your GPS.) There are several freeware programs that do this nicely, along with those made by brand-name software manufacturers. While loading your cache information it is also a good idea to retrieve coordinates and descriptions for a few additional nearby caches that interest you as well. If you find your first cache ahead of schedule you can redirect your attention to another local option. Some caches are close to the road, and it isn't unheard of to do three to four caches in a day.

A critical step, which can be the source of a lot of headaches, is setting up your GPS receiver for the first time. Coordinate systems and mapping datums are discussed in Chapter 7, but before going into too much detail it is important that your GPS and sources of geographic coordinate information match. Geocaching.com displays latitude and longitude as well as Universal Transverse Mercator (UTM) coordinates for every geocache. Latitude/longitude (Lat/Lon) coordinates are displayed in the format of degrees and decimal minutes (DDM), as opposed to degrees, minutes, seconds (DMS) or degrees and decimal degrees (DDD). UTM coordinates do not have these variations and are always displayed in a structure of zones, northings, and eastings. Datums, however, affect all coordinate systems, including Lat/Lon and UTM. The default datum for most GPS receivers is NAD83/WGS84, which refers to the North American Datum of 1983 and the World Geodetic System of 1984. Don't fret, this sounds very complicated, but the bottom line is that your GPS should be set to either Lat/Lon in the format of degrees and decimal minutes or UTM, your choice. The datum on your GPS should be set to WGS84 in order to work correctly with coordinates from Geocaching.com. If you are using any other source of information, whether printed maps, digital maps, or coordinates from a friend, be sure to match the datum or you will not find what you are looking for.

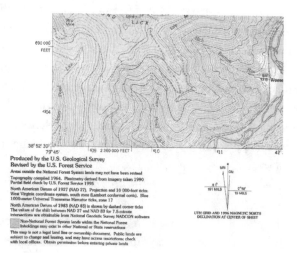

In the bottom left-hand corner of all USGS 7.5-minute topographic maps the datum of each map is listed. In this example, the map is projected in NAD27 but includes dashed corner ticks in NAD83 as well. *(Courtesy of USGS)*

A successful hunt often begins by retrieving small details about the cache prior to heading out. Be sure to note how large the cache is and its description, along with any hiding place hints. Arriving at the cache location and not knowing what you are looking for can make the search process overly daunting. You will see an encrypted sentence on the cache Web site and a deciphering code. By printing the page and taking it with you, you can decipher the hint in the field if you are having a difficult time locating the cache. Be fore-warned that these hints are usually a dead giveaway for the hiding spot and will usually ruin the hunt if you see them before searching. The few times I've been skunked on a search I've reviewed the logs of those who have found it to see if I'm the only one who couldn't. If so, I will make another attempt before using the spoiler. If the object of geocaching is to find a hidden treasure by your skill alone, then, in my mind, using the spoiler is a bit of a defeat.

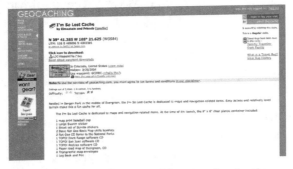

A screen shot, courtesy of Geocaching.com, showing the page of a regular cache game. Each cache has an individual Web site that includes important details about the game, including coordinates, game type, cache contents, and, typically, tips on how to locate it.

Now that you've selected your cache and loaded your GPS unit, it's time to plan your approach to the cache. Begin by using the maps provided on Geocaching.com to get the gist of where you are headed, most importantly the park, town, and other general location aspects.

If you've lived for a while in the area where the cache is hidden you may know the park well and how to get there. For me, an unexpected bonus of the sport has been discovering new driving routes across town and parks that I didn't know existed. If you don't know how to get to a location, a local road map or driving direction Web site such as Mapblast.com or Mapquest.com is the best way to figure it out. If you are using public transportation you may need a route map and timetable as well. If the cache you are looking for is in a large park with multiple access points, the online services will have a distinct advantage by being able to show you the cache location by its coordinate, whereas, more than likely, a road map of your town does not have a coordinate grid that would enable you to plot the cache location. Once the cache is generally pinpointed it is just a matter of choosing the best park access point, the one that is the closest to the cache location and provides the simplest approach. If you used an Internet-based map service, print out the driving directions and keep them handy throughout the trip.

Next, depending on the map resources you have at home, you'll want to plan your hike from your chosen access point to the cache location. Topographic maps are your best source of terrain information and are very helpful when it comes to reading the lay of the land. As mentioned earlier, the USGS topos do not often show the most recent trails. Therefore, you may want to turn to the Web site of the park or other open space that governs the area. Some parks display updated trail maps and information regarding area closures or trail reroutes on the Internet. If not, you can often find printed versions of park maps in a box at the trailhead or as part of a large sign with information, regulations, and other vital park details. Additionally, chambers of commerce and visitor information centers in your town may have racks with local open-space maps; a set for your area is a great resource to have at home. However, be forewarned that these maps do not usually have a coordinate system on them, meaning that pinpointing your cache location on the provided map will be a challenge, if not impossible. The best method to overcome this is to compare the park trail map side-by-side with a topo and then pencil in park trails and your route on the topo. The reason for checking a local trail map is twofold. First, by plotting your cache location and trails you will develop a frame of reference for knowing which trails you should take to get to the cache. Second, assuming you have only loaded the coordinate for the cache itself, remember that a GPS will direct you toward that location as the crow flies; by consulting a local trail map you will be able to find and read other coordinates off of the USGS topo and load them in as a means of ensuring your are on the right path. Choose the best set of trails and roads that enable you to get as close to the cache as possible with the least amount of off-trail travel.

Mapping software such as DeLorme's, Maptech's, and National Geographic's TOPO! really shine during this part of the geocache preparation process. Not only can you plot out the exact path that you'd like to take, the software will automatically load this path into your GPS receiver as a route. Then it's just a matter of printing out a copy of the map with your custom annotations and heading out the door.

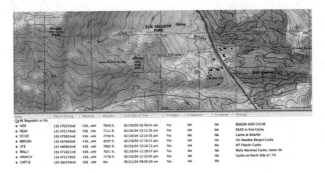

Mapping software, such as National Geographic's TOPO! State Series pictured here, makes loading your GPS easy and planning your day outdoors effortless. *(Courtesy of National Geographic Maps)*

With your GPS loaded, printed geocache page from the Web site, maps, compass, and route in mind, it's time to make one last check of equipment before heading out. Make sure that your GPS has fresh batteries—perhaps carry a set of spares; that you've packed the compass and have water and any snacks for the trail; that you've checked the weather and dressed appropriately for conditions; and, last but not least, that you've let someone know where you are going. Don't forget to pack a little something to place in the cache, and bring along a pen or pencil and a camera if you'd like to snap a few pictures of your find. Now, you're off!

Those who have never geocached assume that it must be a really easy game; after all, your GPS will take you right to the spot where the cache is hidden, right? Wrong! Your GPS will get you very close, but the fun and challenging part of the game is the scrounging around during the last thirty feet or so.

When you arrive at the trailhead pull out your map and follow your planned route toward the cache. If you entered a coordinate for the spot at which you'll need to go off trail, turn on your GPS, let it acquire your location, and then have it "go to" the coordinate. Once activated, your GPS will display something such as an arrow or road, pointing you in the direction to head. Be careful here! GPS receivers know at what point on the Earth you are, but unless you are moving most cannot tell you which way you are facing! Some receivers have built-in compasses, but most do not. A GPS will display a numerical bearing to your destination and an arrow, but more often than not the arrow will not match up to the bearing it is directing you to head. So, my advice is to ignore the GPS when you are at a dead stop. If you want to verify which way to head, simply pull out your compass, turn the dial to the bearing displayed on the GPS receiver, and then turn your entire body until the magnetic needle in the compass lines up with the orienting arrow on the inside of the compass bezel. You are now pointing in the correct direction of your next waypoint. As you start to move the GPS will once again be able to calculate your path and show you the correct way to go. Don't let your GPS lead you astray and make your hike more difficult than it needs to be. If your GPS points in a direction that is different from the way the trail is headed, simply check your trail map and see if the trail switches back or curves around.

Proceed up the trail and occasionally check your map until you reach the point at which you must leave the comfort of the trail to begin your cache search. In some cases, you will never need to venture more than a few feet away, yet, on average, I've found that most caches sit from thirty to one hundred feet off trail. Set your GPS receiver to "go to" the waypoint entered for the geocache, if you haven't done so already, and make note of the bearing and the distance the GPS provides. Now is another opportunity to verify your direction of travel by pulling out the compass, setting the bearing, aligning the needle with the compass bezel, and heading off in the right direction. Once you are moving again, start watching your GPS. When you get within a few tenths of a mile most receivers will alert you that you are approaching your destination. Continue walking along this same bearing until the GPS says you are at the destination with a distance of zero miles left to go. Remember that GPS receivers have an accuracy of roughly thirty feet in radius, so your search area is roughly 2,800 square feet around your current spot. At this point, your GPS has completed its job and can do little more than verify that you are still in the right spot.

Searching for a geocache is often most effective if it is done in a systematic process. There are many ways in which to approach the search, and in some cases elaborate search plans won't be necessary at all because the hiding spot will stick out like a sore thumb. But in those instances when the search becomes a little more challenging, the first step is to define your search area. Standing at the point your GPS says is "the spot," set down your pack or a jacket to serve as a visual reference. Take your GPS and compass and walk in one of the four cardinal directions away from your marked point. Keep an eye on your GPS; when its arrow points directly behind you, toward your jacket, mark this as one edge of the search area. Complete this process to define a box in which the geocache might be. Keep in mind that your GPS is only as accurate as the signal it is receiving, so if you are in a narrow canyon or heavy tree cover take note that your search area may be larger than it appears. Some GPS receivers show estimated point error, or EPE, which is a calculated inaccuracy the GPS receiver believes it has in feet; add this inaccuracy to your search.

More than likely, your first few caches will be simple to find and developing a systematic approach will not be necessary.

Some caches, such as this one, are very easy to spot and do not require further searching. *(Photograph by Mike Dyer)*

For the more challenging searches there are a few things to consider. Caches are rarely left out in the open; they are typically under a pile of rocks, in a hollowed tree branch, under dense brush, or nestled into a crack. If the terrain in your search area is sloped a good technique is to go to the farthest downhill side and work upwards. By having the terrain laid out in front of you at eye level you can see into cracks and under rocks that you wouldn't be able to when approaching from above. Keep in mind what you are looking for as this will certainly narrow down the spots in which the cache is likely hidden. If you see something out of place in nature, such as a stack of rocks, it's a good bet that the cache is hidden there.

A cache located behind a few additional rocks, well concealed in a large crack. *(Photograph by Mike Dyer)*

Finally, be sure to visually sweep your search area prior to walking around in it. This may point out an obvious location to begin your search, but will also give you perspective on how far to search in each direction. If you get confused as to how far or where to look, simply pull out your GPS, get a signal, and then verify your bearing to the cache with your compass.

When searching be careful not to overly disturb the area by trampling. Not only is this a good environmental practice to follow but your disruptions will identify the cache location to future seekers. If you've left any visible tracks, such as disturbed leaves or unsettled dirt, try to disguise your marks before leaving the cache site. For those of us who live in areas with snow, wintertime can make geocaching either extra challenging or very easy. The challenge comes when a cache is buried in snow and may be impossible to find. On the flip side, if you do locate the cache your footprints and dug hole will be the perfect giveaway to future seekers; they might as well not even use their GPS! There really isn't much you can do to effectively disguise your path in snow; it's just a waste of time to try. Frankly, you shouldn't be too concerned about wintertime geocaching; few people do it when there is a lot of snow on the ground, but, more importantly, when deciding which cache to find you can see if someone was just there and weigh the possibility of whether that site may have been spoiled by tracks.

Once you've located your cache make a mental note of how it was hidden because you'll need to put it back exactly the way you found it. Take a moment to read through the log and learn about other people's experiences, then jot down the date, time, your name, and message as verification of your find. In most cases it is customary to take something from the cache and leave something for the next seeker, and you'll find these exchanges logged in the book too. If your cache contains a Travel Bug or other traveling trinket, check the logbook to see if it has a specific goal noted by the previous holder. You can choose to take the bug or leave it; it's really up to you. If you do pack it out, you'll have one more step to complete when logging your cache find on the Web site. Once done, rested, and full of pride from your first cache find, carefully hide the cache back in its original location and replace any covering materials on top of it. Make the shortest path possible back to the trail and head on home, or on to your next cache!

But don't forget that you are not done quite yet. On your computer at home return to the geocaching Web site and log your find, or, if you weren't so lucky, your "couldn't find." In some cases cache owners may request that you e-mail them a password or phrase as proof of finding the cache. Others may not, but this is especially true of virtual caches and some mystery caches when a logbook may not exist and the password serves as your final proof of find. If you did end up taking a traveling trinket, such as a Travel Bug, you will need to secondarily log that you took it from the cache. This is done by browsing through the applicable links to the Travel Bug's Web site and logging that you found the bug. Each bug has a goal, so read about the bug you found and address any individual requirements. The requirements of the Travel Bug may be as simple as taking a picture of it with a certain item or dropping it off at another cache, which may lead it to a location objective. An example: The "I Love Wine" Travel Bug asks to have a picture taken of it with your favorite bottle of wine or winery and then e-mail this picture to the Travel Bug creator before placing it in another cache. Once you've moved the bug to its next cache, you'll want to log on to its page once more and note where you moved it to and when.

Finding other types of caches, such as multi-, offset, or virtual caches, involves the same principles of the traditional games but will test you in other ways. Multicaches will usually test your ability at GPS and land navigation, but simple versions are akin to extended basic games where, instead of finding one cache, you simply find two or three in a row. Offset caches are similar in that same respect yet they involve decrypting a puzzle or finding where to go next based on information displayed at the first location.

Caches that are located in an urban setting can be the most difficult and the most embarrassing cache games to participate in. The urban environment contains many creative hiding spots and there are few that are obvious with nothing but a coordinate.

For example, I completed an urban cache that took me to the parking lot of a large discount retailer. There wasn't an obvious hiding spot to my eyes so I ended up wandering around a landscaped strip, peering under trees, digging through bushes, and feeling into drainpipes. On two instances cars pulled up close to where I was so I ended up pretending that my GPS was a cell phone so that I didn't appear like a complete idiot. It took two trips, deciphering the spoiler, and appearing as a "freak" to countless shoppers before I finally located the crafty hiding spot.

With one find now under your belt, go get some more. Try a variety of cache types and sizes and see how creative some cache designers get. Once you've found half a dozen or so you'll really have the knack for preparation, navigation, and searching. Using your GPS becomes the easiest part of any cache game. As you master your model's functionality any awkwardness you might have had will quickly fade away and the focus and skill of the game will become solving unique cache games and searching an area riddled with hiding spots.

While I stated that the last thirty feet of any cache game are the most difficult, many caches are very easy to find. You may even wonder why some caches haven't simply "walked away" because they are hidden in plain site. For the more well-hidden caches there really aren't surefire, step-by-step directions I can provide, beyond the tips I've already given, other than to reiterate the importance of planning your approach, defining the search area, and then looking for the obvious before beginning a systematic survey of the area.

# Chapter 6
## Creating Your First Cache

Building and hiding your first cache is no harder than finding one, it simply requires different preparation. Chances are you already have a great idea of where to hide your cache; it may be a park you frequent or a concept for a cool puzzle game. To get the hang of the process, a traditional cache is the easiest to create and requires the least amount of preparation. Before getting too far ahead of the game, your first step is to verify that your great spot meets the rules and guidelines regarding where you can legally place a geocache. You can flip back to the last chapter of this book for a short list of guidelines but, more importantly, check with the group or Web site you plan on posting this cache with to ensure you meet their individual requirements. Finally, seek approval from the group that manages the land where you plan on hiding your cache. It is currently safe to say that USFS and BLM land is A-OK, but all other parks and managed lands may have their own ordinances. In general, caches should not be located in or on:

- National parks
- National monuments
- Nature preserves or wildlife management areas
- Military installations
- Private property
- Areas cordoned off for environmental impact protection
- Sensitive ecological areas where foot traffic would cause harm
- Areas where activity might cause alarm

If your desired location does not fall under any of these categories you are safe to place your cache. However, I'd encourage you to locate your cache in a spot where seekers can do the bulk of their navigation on trail and limit the amount of cross-country travel to a minimum.

Once you've selected your site, the second step is to select the type of cache game and size of the cache you wish to hide. The size of your cache is often controlled by the size of your hiding spot, but certainly a microcache can be hidden anywhere, while a large cache requires a very specific location to accommodate its girth. When choosing your cache size another consideration is whether you want to put items into your cache for trade. If so, this rules out most microcaches, for you are not going to fit much more than a logbook and perhaps a golf pencil inside a film canister.

Once you've selected which type of cache game you want to make and the size of the cache, the next step is construction. Cache boxes can be made of anything, but the most popular items are sealable, plastic containers and ammo boxes.

Ammo boxes, such as this one, are very common for regular cache games due to their durability, waterproof qualities, size, and value. *(Photograph by Mike Dyer)*

Both are readily available at big box discount stores, but you may stand a better chance of locating an ammo box at an army surplus store or hunting shop. When selecting the container, evaluate its durability and, especially, whether the container is watertight. Caches will be exposed to all the elements and a weak lid will allow moisture in and destroy the container's contents. Inexpensive plastic food containers may have a good seal but they crack more easily than a more pliable rubber container. In addition to simply keeping the cache items dry, the box must stand up to a lot of handling and being pulled in and out of hiding spots.

To fill your cache, begin with the logbook. Remember, a log is required in all cache games except for in the few instances described earlier. Good logbooks tend to be small notepads, no larger than three inches by five inches, with at least fifty to one hundred sheets of paper. Outdoor recreation stores sell waterproof notepads for a few dollars more than plain paper ones, but a frugal means of keeping the log dry is to place it in a ziplock bag. When making a microcache you'll need to get creative to develop a log because space is very limited. I once saw a log made out of foot-long, one-inch-wide strips of white paper stapled at the top and rolled to fit into a film canister, which was great. Be sure to kick off your logbook with your own entry and directions if you want finders to do or log anything in particular when they've found your cache.

A few other ingredients should be added to all caches, regardless of size. First, although a writing implement is not necessary, it is generally expected. If your cache can't physically hold a pen or pencil, make a note on the Web site informing seekers to carry one of their own. If you want additional verification that someone found your cache you may want to include a password written on your logbook cover or on a separate piece of paper. For those extremely tiny caches too small for a logbook, including a password on a scrap of paper may be the only way to verify that someone visited the cache. Finally, in the event that a nongeocacher stumbles across your cache, be sure to label the outside of the box with "Geocache," the cache's nickname, Web site or applicable club name, and the date it was hidden. Geocaching.com has created a stock letter that explains to someone unfamiliar with the game what they've found and what to do with it; this letter is downloadable from the Web site. Print out a copy and place it inside your cache or else someone may walk off with it.

Most geocaches are designed to be large enough to serve as exchanges for trinkets. That said, next comes the fun part of the cache: stocking it with the initial goodies. What you fill the cache box with is entirely up to your creativity and generosity. Cache items can be of a specific genre, for example paperback books or coins. Or, you may just have a lot of miscellaneous little trinkets you've been eagerly waiting to find a use for. Whatever you decide to use, be smart and do not put any food, alcohol, drugs, or any other dangerous item into your cache.

The next phase is to place your cache in the wild, and this is very similar to finding a cache in reverse. With the completed cache box in hand and your trusty GPS receiver by your side, head out to your desired hiding spot. Be certain that the location of your cache will not create any stress on the landscape, such as placing it on a very steep, dry slope where erosion will surely take place under seekers' feet. When placing your cache you may want to add additional materials to conceal it. For example, you could include some rocks or downed branches, but be respectful of the land and don't overdo your fabrication. There are plenty of great places to hide your cache that do not require disrupting nature.

There are plenty of fantastic hiding spots that require little to no modification. This cache hiding spot is nearly impossible to find when approached from uphill and requires no additional camouflage. *(Photographs by Mike Dyer)*

After the cache has been hidden, take out your GPS and wait for a good signal. The more satellites your GPS is interfacing with the higher the accuracy of the location. Wait until you have an absolute minimum of three satellites, but preferably more, before marking the position. A good technique for verifying the position of your hiding place is to walk away and then use the GPS to navigate back to the cache. If you find that the location this method leads you to is significantly different from where the cache is hidden, mark the cache location again and repeat the process. This is especially necessary if you do not have a clear view of the sky and are in dense tree cover or a narrow canyon. By verifying the position, you give your cache seekers the best possible coordinate and the highest probability of a successful find. Cover your tracks, make sure the area is not disturbed, and head back to your computer.

The final step is to post your cache, a simple and painless process. If you use Geocaching.com you will work through an online form, first by selecting the cache type and size, and then providing the box's coordinates. Next, you will provide two descriptions of the game and hidden cache; one is a short summary, the other is a detailed description—how detailed is up to you. Finally, you will create an encrypted hint for those who are having difficulty finding your hiding spot. I suggest offering a good clue but don't blatantly give the hiding spot away. For a cache I recently hid in an old tree stump my hint was "I was provided many years of shade." Carefully review all of the information you have provided and double-check your coordinates. Don't forget to make sure your datum matches as well.

Posting a new cache is as simple as filling out this form on Geocaching.com. *(Courtesy of Geocaching.com)*

After it is submitted your cache will be reviewed prior to posting, and, barring any obvious broken rules, it will be posted in a couple of days. As the cache creator it will now be your responsibility to manage the cache, including editing the data on the Web site, adding any pictures later on, or, in the worst case scenario, taking it down. Due to the growing number of geocache participants, it won't be long before the cache is visited and you'll receive your first confirmation e-mail. As you continue to receive notifications of successful or unsuccessful finds, be sure to read the comments and take any action you may need to correct problems. One of my caches recently outgrew its box, so I needed to head out and "super size" the container. Another had a camera that ran out of film, so I replaced it with a new one, and while I was there, provided a new logbook and pen. It is important to know that hiding your cache is only the first step to a longer-term commitment of maintenance.

Creating a multi- or offset cache requires more work than a traditional cache game, but the rewards include a more sophisticated and challenging hunt. Let's review how these games work, as this will provide you with a vision for how to create a game of either type. To complete an offset cache you are provided with the coordinates to a specific place—usually a marker, plaque, statue, tombstone, etc. Along with the coordinates for the first part of the cache, the creator provides a riddle or a decryption table of some fashion that references data found on the information source. For example, you may be directed to find a statue and on the base of the statue is the name of the figure. Using his name and a decryption table that converts the letters of his name into numbers, you'll decipher enough to learn the coordinate, bearing, or other navigational aid to the final cache location.

Similar to creating a basic cache, to create an offset cache you'll need a cache box, logbook, information sheet, and any goodies you want to put up for trade. But the additional step will be to go to the information source and conjure up a riddle or problem based on its content. However, you'll need to know the coordinate of the final cache location prior to doing so. Therefore, the sequence of events will take you to the starting point last, after you've carefully hidden the cache and retrieved its accurate position. Then you'll head to the beginning, reacquire an accurate GPS signal, and mark the location of the information source. Remember, on the Web site for an offset cache you do not provide the coordinate to the cache box itself, only the coordinate to the location where the seeker must solve your riddle. But you will need the coordinate of the final cache box for calculating your riddle and also when it comes time for posting on the Web site for approval. When posting an offset cache, you will provide both coordinates for the approval process to ensure that neither location breaks any set posting guidelines.

A multicache requires finding one cache box after another, each containing a clue to finding the next cache. The clue can simply be the coordinate to the next cache, a bearing, or a riddle that, when deciphered, reveals another navigational aid. They are usually found in sequence, but not always, as in the case of the triangulation multicache I mentioned as an example earlier in the book. To create a multicache you will need to build one final cache box with similar contents to that of the basic cache game (logbook, information sheet, and goodies), as well as several other caches that will only contain the geographic directions to the next box in the sequence. Similar to the offset cache, you should begin by hiding the final cache box, acquiring a good signal, and marking its coordinate. Then go to the location where you wish to place the second to last cache box. Before hiding it, be sure to include the coordinate or bearing to the final cache box inside of it, mark its coordinate, and so on. On the Web site you'll post the multicache to the site, once again providing coordinates to all hidden caches in the game for approval purposes, but only the starting cache will be revealed to the public.

Mystery caches require preparation very similar to that of offset and multicache types, however much more time will be spent developing your puzzle. As you'll recall, a mystery cache provides the seeker with a coordinate to a general location, for example to a parking lot, and also provides a complex puzzle or riddle to solve based on the surroundings that the seeker is in. To develop your mystery game, once again you will start by choosing the location of the final cache and collecting its coordinate. Then you must select the general starting point, which has enough "character" to create a puzzle that will reveal the final cache's location. The only specific requirement to mystery caches is that the starting point is no farther than two miles from the final cache spot. This is to ensure that distances calculated for Travel Bugs are not significantly miscalculated.

To illustrate a mystery cache game, imagine that you have just arrived at a large parking lot; you've navigated here with the provided coordinates and are now tasked with solving the following riddle:

> The cache is within walking distance, you are almost there. Studying the place you are, answer the following questions in order. Your correct answers will reveal the latitude and longitude of the final cache. Good luck! How many parking spaces are in the lot? How many lamps are on the east side of the lot? How many letters are in the name of the store? There is a large Dumpster on the south side of the building, how many letters are in the name of its color? Standing at the door to the store and facing the parking lot, how many letters are in the direction you are facing? When you've figured these out, you're ready to find the cache.

Assuming someone correctly completes a set of questions such as this, they'll end up with the coordinate for the cache and move on to find it.

Thus, when creating a mystery cache be prepared to spend a fair amount of time at the starting point studying the surroundings and crafting your puzzle. Since creativity is the key to all caches, these puzzles can take many forms, far beyond the simple set of questions illustrated above. You may require that someone learn a little local history to answer your questions or figure out some complex math. Whatever you fancy, remember the main objective is that someone will go to a spot, solve a riddle from the surroundings, and move on.

Out of all cache types, virtual caches require the least amount of preparation because the creator is simply sharing the view of an incredible location by providing coordinates to it. Generally, all you need to do is go to the location, collect a quality coordinate, and know the view of the feature that is at the spot, then proceed to the Web site and post it. A virtual cache must be a place that has a significant "wow" factor, meaning that a statue in a local park is unacceptable, but a jaw-dropping view of the ocean, caves with incredible Native art, or an epic natural feature would suffice just fine. When someone finds the virtual cache location they see the view that you, as the cache creator, intended for them and then, as proof, must report what they saw by photo or detailed description. When you submit a virtual cache for approval it is a good idea to include a picture of the "wow" factor and describe to the reviewer why this is so special, if it isn't obvious. Virtual caches are the only type of cache that can skirt some of the placement restrictions in protected areas, such as national parks. A great virtual cache location might be the top of Half Dome in Yosemite or the base of Niagara Falls.

Letterboxing is a sport similar to geocaching, as described earlier, and, for our purposes as geocachers, we call the modified game a letterbox hybrid. This game, versus any other form, is the closest to creating a traditional geocache game but has a few simple twists. First, a letterbox game requires a rubber stamp. The stamp can be anything, as long as it is unique, for example a "copy" stamp from your office is not very creative. Hallmark stores, craft stores, and, ideally, rubber stamp or scrapbooking shops are where you should choose the mark for your cache. Next, hide the cache and retrieve a

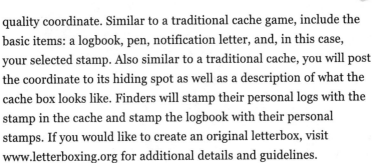

quality coordinate. Similar to a traditional cache game, include the basic items: a logbook, pen, notification letter, and, in this case, your selected stamp. Also similar to a traditional cache, you will post the coordinate to its hiding spot as well as a description of what the cache box looks like. Finders will stamp their personal logs with the stamp in the cache and stamp the logbook with their personal stamps. If you would like to create an original letterbox, visit www.letterboxing.org for additional details and guidelines.

Creating a webcam cache is similar to creating a virtual cache, but it does require a bit more preliminary research. The object of this game is to have someone send in a picture of him or herself taken by a webcam in a public place. Good examples of this are traffic webcams or live cams posted in a popular downtown location. To create a webcam cache, begin by searching the Internet for Web pages of cameras in your town. Once you've located the camera, you'll need to dig around on its Web site and make sure that, knowing a specific date and time, someone can retrieve an archived picture from that Web page. If the site has a page that meets these criteria, then your next step is to go the camera and collect an accurate coordinate of its location. Posting the cache is simple; it involves providing the coordinate and perhaps a sample webcam picture. Since this game type does not include a logbook or even a physical cache, as proof that the person found the cache you may wish that a seeker hold their GPS in view on the webcam picture they submit or do something silly such as hold up their right hand and place their left hand on their head. Personally, I have not participated in this game because I have yet to find a webcam in my area that has the ability to display archived images instead of only real-time pictures. But they sound like a lot of fun to create, and you could certainly have fun making the cache's finder do something funny in a public place.

Last but not least are locationless, or reverse, caches. Unlike every other cache type, a locationless cache does not provide a coordinate to go to, nor is there a physical cache to find. Similar to benchmark hunting, the seeker is merely provided with an object to find and then reports the coordinates of those objects once they've been found. An example would be to visit and report on the highest point of elevation in every county in the United States. In this case, the searcher would first do some research as to where that point is, travel to it, collect the coordinate, and then provide a description of what was there and perhaps a picture as well. Locationless caching is very similar to a scavenger hunt where, instead of playing the typical hide-and-go-seek game, the player is given a list of specific real-world items to find versus a purposefully hidden cache box.

To create one of these games you should begin by choosing an object that has mass distribution and that would apply far outside of your local area. A good example would be locating swing sets or McDonald's restaurants. Next, find one of these items in your local area, take a picture of it, and decide if you want seekers to tell you anything specific or do anything at the ones they find. The final step is to post the locationless cache on the Web site. Include a picture of the object and describe what people are to find. Certainly, there are not the same rules and guidelines for placing a locationless cache, but be sure to select an item that is not going to lead to problems, such as collecting coordinates of freeway overpasses, airport terminals, banks, or other areas where using a GPS and a digital camera would cause alarm.

Creating a geocache varies a lot depending on the type of game you are developing and can be manipulated by your own imagination. Open your mind to what concoction of a geocache game you can create. I'll stress again that the best way to get going is to start by creating a traditional cache. With the experience you'll gain by building a cache box and working through the various online processes, any hesitation you might have had about creating your own game will vanish. Next time you are out on a hike or driving in your car, keep an eye out for a place you'd like to explore or a great cache location that simply jumps out at you. Create a cache and hide it there. Going through these simple steps will make the process seem less daunting and will get your creative juices flowing.

# Chapter 7
# A Geocacher's Guide to Land Navigation

Geocaching is a fantastic sport in which GPS users can hone their navigational skills and have fun while doing it. Geocaching can be an incredible teaching tool for a product that is often labeled as difficult and unwieldy to use. In the GPS clinics and classes that I've both taught and learned from, the greatest challenge faced by the instructor is to make GPS easy to understand without overwhelming the students with jargon. Geocaching can make basic GPS functionality very easy to understand. The steps of loading a coordinate, navigating to a coordinate, and marking your location are the three essentials that make up the backbone of geocaching. But, although these simple steps cover the fundamentals of GPS use, I strongly believe that it is important to have a thorough understanding of navigational principles, including map reading and interpretation, along with basic orienteering principles, in order to completely and safely use your receiver in all outdoor activities. With that said, this chapter is meant to be a bridge; the goal is to teach you the core values of land navigation, building on the three basic skills you've learned from geocaching.

To begin learning about land navigation you need to start with the foundation: maps. In geocaching you will use a variety of map types, including topographic, general reference (road maps), and thematic (trails at a park). Supposedly, every map requires a few key elements such as scale, projection, and accurately georeferenced content. Yet all of us have created maps on napkins, for example, that have sufficed to provide specific directions, or used free trail maps generated by a local park that do not include all of these requisites. Therefore, your first step when working with maps is to evaluate *what* you are working with or, more technically speaking, the accuracy of the map.

Maps published by any of the major mapping companies, such as National Geographic, DeLorme, Rand McNally, AAA, and government agencies such as the USGS and National Oceanic and Atmospheric Association (NOAA), abide by strict rules for accuracy. But with the advent of desktop publishing nearly anyone with enough prowess to place some lines on a page can make a beautiful map that *appears* accurate. My cartography teacher at San Francisco State University was one of the most detailed—and frankly, anal—men I've ever met, and I mean that in the nicest way. At least once a week he'd bring in a beautiful map from somewhere and post it in the classroom, offering ten extra-credit points to those who could pick out five or more flaws. Few could do it, even those of us who had spent hours studiously sitting through cartography seminars and instruction. The real value of the assignment, though, was that it opened our minds and required us, as budding cartographers, to hold a strict line to quality and abide by the long-standing rules of cartography.

As geocachers, one challenge we face is the availability of quality trail maps for the places we wish to go. For our needs, the ideal map is one that has topographic information, updated trails and roads, as well as an easy-to-read coordinate system for locating geographic coordinates in the field. Sadly, our wish list is hard to fulfill in one map. The USGS has, by far, the best topographical information, but their maps are not always updated regularly. Private topo maps, such as those made by Trails Illustrated, are perfect for our needs, but their coverage is somewhat limited. And the free trail maps from parks usually have the most accurate trail information but often are not accurate for scale, nor do they provide any coordinates to cross-reference to output from a GPS receiver or the position of a geocache. Therefore, the best skill to hone is being able to read and interpret a variety of maps and combine their positive attributes into a thorough understanding of an area. For geocaching and other outdoor endeavors the USGS topographic map is the

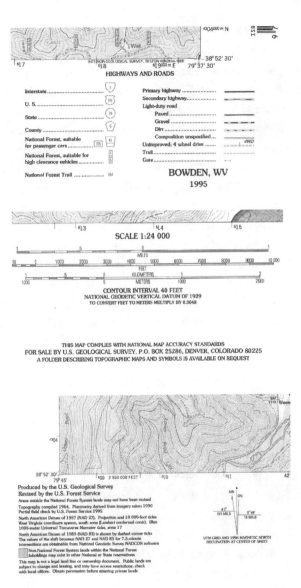

HIGHWAYS AND ROADS

| | | | |
|---|---|---|---|
| Interstate | | Primary highway | |
| | | Secondary highway | |
| U.S. | | Light-duty road | |
| | | Paved | |
| State | | Gravel | |
| | | Dirt | |
| County | | Composition unspecified | |
| National Forest, suitable for passenger cars | | Unimproved; 4 wheel drive | 4WD |
| | | Trail | |
| National Forest, suitable for high clearance vehicles | | Gate | |
| National Forest Trail | | | |

**BOWDEN, WV**
1995

**SCALE 1:24 000**

MILES

FEET

KILOMETERS

METERS

**CONTOUR INTERVAL 40 FEET**
NATIONAL GEODETIC VERTICAL DATUM OF 1929
TO CONVERT FEET TO METERS MULTIPLY BY 0.3048

THIS MAP COMPLIES WITH NATIONAL MAP ACCURACY STANDARDS
FOR SALE BY U.S. GEOLOGICAL SURVEY, P.O. BOX 25286, DENVER, COLORADO 80225
A FOLDER DESCRIBING TOPOGRAPHIC MAPS AND SYMBOLS IS AVAILABLE ON REQUEST

Produced by the U.S. Geological Survey
Revised by the U.S. Forest Service
Areas outside the National Forest System lands may not have been revised
Topography compiled 1964. Planimetry derived from imagery taken 1990
Partial field check by U.S. Forest Service 1995
North American Datum of 1927 (NAD 27). Projection and 10 000-foot ticks:
West Virginia coordinate system, south zone (Lambert conformal conic). Blue
1000-meter Universal Transverse Mercator ticks, zone 17
North American Datum of 1983 (NAD 83) is shown by dashed corner ticks
The values of the shift between NAD 27 and NAD 83 for 7.5-minute
intersections are obtainable from National Geodetic Survey NADCON software
Non-National Forest System lands within the National Forest
Inholdings may exist in other National or State reservations
This map is not a legal land line or ownership document. Public lands are
subject to change and leasing, and may have access restrictions; check
with local offices. Obtain permission before entering private lands

UTM GRID AND 1996 MAGNETIC NORTH
DECLINATION AT CENTER OF SHEET

Shown in the three images here, the bottom of every USGS
7.5-minute quad contains critical information including
scale, contour interval, symbol key, and adjoining maps.
*(Courtesy of USGS)*

source of base data for most maps, private and government, and is where we'll begin and focus our study.

When beginning to read any map, including topographic maps, the first place to start is the "instructions," in other words, the information contained in the margins, known appropriately as marginalia. In the margins you'll find publication and revision dates, scale in the form of either a numeric or a graphic display such as a scale bar, geographic coordinates, the map name and adjoining map names, contour interval, north arrow and magnetic declination diagram, a legend, and, in some cases, a glossary. Since all maps are not alike it is important to read and understand the marginalia before making any assumptions based on previous maps you've encountered, even if they are from the same publisher. USGS 7.5-minute topographic maps, for example, contain varied contour intervals, magnetic declinations, and, in some cases, even represent geographic coordinate systems differently, yet many people overlook these differences.

## Reading Topographic Maps

Topographic maps—the most useful maps for geocaching—use lines of equal elevation, called contours, to show the shape of the land. Since all points along a contour line represent the same elevation above sea level, contour lines will never cross one another. On USGS topos contour lines are usually brown and, in most cases, are some of the most prominent features on the map, although they are less clearly defined in very flat areas. Every fourth or fifth contour line is wider than the others and is referred to as an index contour. Index contours numerically display the elevation they represent at various points staggered across the map. The difference in elevation between any two contour lines is its contour interval, which can be located at the bottom center of every USGS topographic map near the scale bar (see the previous figure). Contour intervals vary on quadrangles depending on the terrain the map is representing. Areas that are flat may have a contour interval of ten feet or less, while steep terrain may require a contour interval of one hundred feet between lines in order to correctly depict the shape of the land versus the scale of the map and sheet size. Finding the elevation of any point is as simple as locating the closest numbered index contour and then adding or subtracting the contour interval for each contour line between the index contour and your point of interest.

With such a large number of contour lines, reading a topographic map can be confusing, but there are a few simple tricks that will help you visualize the terrain. First, the closer the contour lines —in some cases they are so close you can barely make out that they are separated—the steeper the slope they represent. The opposite is true for flatter areas; the contour lines are spaced farther and farther apart the flatter the terrain gets.

Water, shown in cyan on USGS maps, can be a great aid as well. Keep in mind that water always runs downhill—if for some reason this fact changes we're in deep trouble! When reading a topographic map you will notice that contour lines bend around streams and rivers creating a U or V shape. The point of the V always points uphill.

The figure above shows how contour lines bend around streams creating Vs and always point up hill. Black arrows are added to this image to help demonstrate. *(Map image courtesy of National Geographic TOPO! State Series)*

This trick can be very helpful when reading a map of rolling terrain where lots of valleys, mounds, and small hills can make it challenging to stay oriented. One advantage to the topographic software products is their terrain modeling features, which range from shaded relief to full-blown three-dimensional capabilities, such as in the DeLorme and Maptech products. While certainly not a necessity, adding shaded relief or creating a three-dimensional image is a great way to learn how to read topography and, more importantly, to visualize terrain.

In geocaching the skill of reading topography becomes beneficial during the planning process of finding a cache and essential the more remote the cache is. When you can look at a topo and "see" the terrain before you, it enables you to trace out an approach that requires the least amount of exertion, whether that be avoiding steep slopes, marshy areas, or deep canyons that may impact GPS reception.

In addition to contour lines and streams, topographic maps show vegetation, bodies of water, boundaries, and man-made items such as roads, trails, and even some buildings. Important geodetic data points, such as benchmarks, are also depicted on the maps, which makes USGS topos an awesome tool for benchmark hunting. There are too many symbols to discuss here, but there are several ways to obtain a complete list. Early USGS topos contained a complete symbol guide on the back of each map, but today this guide is available as a free pamphlet from the USGS. It can be downloaded from their Web site or obtained in a printed version from your map retailer or from a USGS Earth Science Information Center (ESIC). Most privately made topos, such as National Geographic's Trails Illustrated, have symbol legends printed directly on the maps.

Besides showing elevation, all USGS topographic maps are carefully georeferenced to several coordinate systems, which makes them extremely useful for our purposes as GPS users. While geocaches provide us with a coordinate of the hiding spot, for planning purposes and endeavors outside of the geocache game we, as technological navigators, need to find coordinates for new locations, and this is accomplished by reading coordinates from a map.

Before diving into how to do this, let's discuss a few basics regarding maps and their relation to Earth. The greatest challenge of any cartographer is creating a two-dimensional, flat image of our three-dimensional, round world, and thus creating an accurate system to pinpoint where you are in relation to other places on the globe. It is due to this challenge that coordinate systems were developed, and the most common is latitude and longitude.

Imagine the world as an orange, with each segment divided by a set of lines running vertically from north to south; these are the lines of longitude, which are measured in terms of degrees from 0° to 360°. Conversely, there are lines of latitude, which run perpendicular to lines of longitude and range from 0° to 90° north and south of the equator. Since most people neither navigate across the globe in a single leap nor calculate global distances often, both latitude and longitude are divided into halves commonly referred to as hemispheres. The eastern and western longitudinal hemispheres are defined between 0°, which happens to run through Greenwich, England, and 180°, the International Date Line (IDL). Degrees of longitude increase in both directions from 0°, and, to keep from confusing which degree of longitude you are referring to, all longitudes include a cardinal direction, or name of the hemisphere, for which they belong. For example, New York City lies at roughly 75° west longitude, while Bombay, India, lies at 75° east longitude. Latitude works in a similar fashion, except it is divided into northern and southern hemispheres with 0° at the equator and 90° at the North and South Poles.

The simplest and least accurate coordinates you can provide are the rough degrees of longitude and latitude for a given point, for example 110° W, 38° N. To provide a more accurate coordinate, say, one good enough to find a geocache, these large aggregates must be broken down further into minutes and seconds. Similar to keeping time, there are sixty minutes in a degree and sixty seconds in minute. As navigators, a more familiar coordinate to us would be 110°38'26" W, 38°15'47" N. There are other variations on degrees, minutes, and seconds as well, and you've surely encountered these on your GPS receiver. Degrees and decimal of degrees (DDD) and degrees and decimal of minutes (DDM) are simply calculated versions of the basic degrees, minutes, and seconds, none of which are more accurate than the other.

Finding a Lat/Lon coordinate on a topo map requires math and some basic tools: at minimum, a calculator, ruler with centimeters, and a pencil. There are also a variety of prefab tools available for finding a coordinate, which make this process much easier, but I believe you should learn the basic way in case you don't have one of these cheats handy. USGS topographic maps are defined by either 7.5 minutes of latitude and longitude or 15 minutes (if you can still find them; the USGS stopped making the 15-minute series in the early '60s). Therefore, each quadrangle covers 7.5 minutes of latitude north to south and 7.5 minutes of longitude east to west. You might expect, then, that a USGS topo would be square, but think again. Remember that the Earth is round, and, once again, imagine the orange if it helps to enlighten you on my description. The lines of longitude meet at the Poles, tapering together just like the segments of the orange. Therefore, maps with coverage defined by Lat and Lon will be as close to square as possible at the equator and get progressively narrower as you approach the Poles. A common question is how much land is covered on a 7.5-minute USGS topo? The honest answer is that it depends on where in the United States you are. In southern Florida the maps will contain significantly more square miles as opposed to those in Nome, Alaska.

Each 7.5-minute USGS topo has four neatlines on the map,

which create the bounding box that divides marginalia from the map data itself. Each neatline is a line of either longitude, on the left and right side, or latitude, on the top and bottom, and between them is 7.5 minutes. The USGS divides the map further into nine 2.5-by-2.5-minute sections, with tick marks shown on the neatlines and corresponding crosshairs on the map itself. The first step to finding a coordinate is to carefully and accurately connect the tick marks and crosshairs to divide the map into nine sections; be sure to mark your lines all the way out to the edge of the paper, across the margin, being as accurate as possible and preferably using an extremely sharp pencil. You'll understand why in a minute.

Next comes some basic math and use of your ruler. Each one of the nine sections you created is a 2'30" square, or a 150" square if you prefer (by multiplying the 2' by 60 and adding the remaining 30"). Using any ruler with equal divisions of 150 we can now find the coordinate for any point you desire. A ruler with a scale up to 30 centimeters works perfectly since 30 divides evenly into 150. Pick a spot on a topo for practice, perhaps the top of a summit or intersection, and locate the two drawn parallels of latitude and the two drawn meridians of longitude that bound this object.

Beginning with latitude, place the "0" mark of your 30-cm ruler on the parallel below the point and then angle the ruler until the "30-cm" mark rests on the parallel directly above. Be sure that the "0" and "30-cm" marks of your ruler remain precisely on your drawn parallel lines and then slide the ruler left to right until your desired object lines up with the centimeters on your ruler, and then take down this number.

Next, take your measured number and multiply it by 5. (Since there are 150" in between the two parallel lines, and we are measuring them with an increment of 30, each centimeter represents 5".) Assuming your object lined up with the "20-cm" mark, this would equate to 20 x 5 = 100. To get the accurate latitude, you will simply

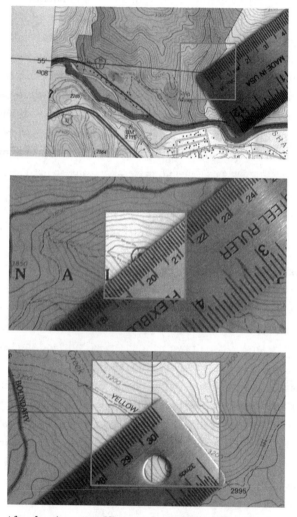

After drawing a set of lines on the USGS map, line up a ruler using the centimeter increments. Carefully place the "0-cm" mark and "30-cm" mark of the ruler on the lines of latitude directly above and below your point of interest. Then simply read the centimeter measurement from the ruler where your point lies; in this example it's 20 centimeters. *(Photographs by Mike Dyer)*

calculate the number of minutes and seconds this equates to using 60 as your divisor. In this example you will have 1'40".

Finally, go back to your topographic map. Find the latitude line below your object and read its coordinate from the marginalia, then add 1'40" to this number. Let's assume that the parallel below your point was 32°15' N, your calculated latitude for your point would be 32°16'40" N.

The process is the same for finding a longitudinal coordinate, but always remember to put the "0" mark on your ruler with the parallel or meridian line with the lowest value. Here in the United States, you'll find your ruler upside down, with the "0" being on the right meridian and the "30" on the left meridian. Since the geographic area covered between these meridians of longitude is the same as it was between the parallels of latitude, you will still multiply your found result by 5. This process for finding an accurate Lat/Lon coordinate is reliant upon the accuracy of the lines drawn connecting the tick marks on our map and the careful alignment of your ruler. Take your time; it is wise to double-check your calculations before heading out into the field.

As you can see, finding a coordinate on a paper map can be time consuming, especially for your first few tries. Imagine planning out a multiday backpacking trip and needing twenty or thirty coordinates to plan a GPS route. What a headache! But by understanding the rudimentary math and means by which to locate Lat/Lon coordinates, you'll be a better geographer. I'd suggest breaking out an old topo and practicing this concept by finding coordinates on different sections of the map. You'll see that having the extended pencil lines on the margin will be a great benefit as you attempt to find a coordinate closer to the neatlines. After you've got the hang of finding a coordinate, I'd suggest investing in a grid tool; it will make your life much easier and only costs a few dollars. Better yet, get yourself a good topographic mapping software application, which will be

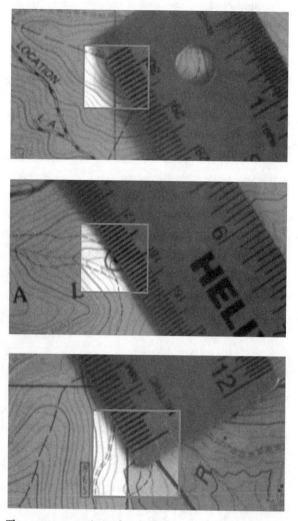

The same process is used to find a longitude, but remember to place the "0" mark on your ruler on the meridian with the lowest value. Here in the United States this will result in your ruler being upside down compared to the map. *(Photographs by Mike Dyer)*

faster and far more accurate than either system.

The concept for finding a Lat/Lon coordinate is the same for any type of map, whether it is a topographic map made by another company or a road map, except you may need to tailor your math and your measurement device depending on how they divided their geographic coordinates. If by chance you are using a map that has tick marks in three-minute increments, for example, your ruler will be dissecting 180" instead of 150". Therefore, when it comes to the final calculations you would need to multiply by 6 (180/30), instead of 5.

Finding a location on a map with a known coordinate employs the same principles but in reverse. We'll use the following coordinate to illustrate how this is done, beginning with locating the latitude 38°15'20" N, 120°20'10" W.

- First, find the geographic lines between which the latitude above falls. Lets assume it's 38°15' and 38°17'30".
- Next, subtract the latitude, 38°15'20", from the larger of the two parallels; in this case it's 38°17'30". This will equal a difference of 2'10", or 130".
- Convert 130 into centimeters. To accomplish this, divide by 5; this equals 26 centimeters.
- Place the "0" cm mark of your ruler anywhere along the 38°15' parallel, the bottom parallel bounding your object, and the "30" cm mark of your ruler on the 39°17'30" parallel. Then place a mark at the 26th centimeter.
- Keeping the "0" and "30" on these parallels, move a few inches to the left or right and repeat the step above.
- Draw an extended line through your two dots. This line represents 38°15'20".

To find the longitude repeat the process above, except use the two meridians that bound your coordinate instead of the latitude parallels. Your position will be where the longitude and latitude lines you've drawn intersect.

This process will be the same with any map you use, regardless of scale or whether the divisions between minutes are larger or smaller than the 2.5 minutes in this example. Just be sure to modify your divisor and adjust your ruler accordingly.

If after hours of practice and carefully drawn pencil lines you still feel lost by latitude and longitude, then there are several other coordinate systems you may find easier, and for most people the choice is Universal Transverse Mercator (UTM). UTM is an entirely different geographic coordinate system, which has a similar history to GPS. After World War II most non-Communist bloc nations agreed to develop a new uniform map location system based on the metric system, instead of latitude and longitude, or, in many cases, odd regional-, state-, or even city-based systems that caused confusion during the war. UTM can be very helpful to a geocacher because it solves a simple problem: knowing how far you are from a position you are trying to reach. Since latitude and longitude have no given relation to distance and are mathematically based on division of the Earth, asking a simple question such as "How far is a second?" results in infinite answers, since the distance will change as you get closer to or farther from the equator. In UTM, positions are generated from a simple metric grid. Positions are shown in meters, which are a constant measure of distance. If you know that you are ten meters from the geocache, you can estimate 30', whereas 2" might you leave you reaching for your calculator or just scratching your head.

Unlike Lat/Lon, UTM does not cover the entire globe but instead ranges between 80° S and 84° N latitude, with its origination point at the intersection of 80° S and 180° (E or W), also known as the International Date Line. There is a version of UTM that covers the Poles, referred to as UPS—not to be confused with the shipping company. However, since few of us will be geocaching there I'll skip over that system, but understand that it works in a similar fashion to UTM. There are two versions of UTM in use worldwide today: the original international version, which is used by everyone abroad as well as the U.S. military, and a nonmilitary version used here in the United States.

The U.S. nonmilitary version extends from 80° S to 80° N latitude, cutting off 4° approaching the Arctic Circle. In UTM, the world is first carved up into zones, beginning at the International Date Line and heading east, circumnavigating the globe and returning back to the IDL. The U.S. system divides the globe into sixty zones north and south from the equator. Each zone covers 6° of longitude and is numbered 1–60. The concept behind UTM is that people rarely need to know or navigate to coordinates outside of their particular zone, and thus portions of the complete written coordinate can be omitted for they are implied. Each zone has a point of origin from which coordinates emanate, and the point of origin starts over from zone to zone. UTM coordinates include a zone number, the hemisphere it lies in (north or south of the equator), as well as the meters east ("easting" from the point of origin in that zone) and the meters north ("northing" from the equator). An example of a UTM coordinate in the U.S. nonmilitary system would appear as 560,300 meters E; 4,208,560 meters N; zone 11, N. In layman terms this would read as 560,300 meters east of the point of origin inside zone 11 (north) and 4,208,560 meters north of the equator. If someone were to give you a coordinate that had the same easting as the example above but 4,208,600 meters northing, you would be able to quickly compute that this position is directly north of your current spot by 40 meters, or roughly 120'. It's that easy.

The international system is very similar and just as easy to use, and more importantly to us as geocachers, it's the system displayed on Geocaching.com. In this version of the system, the UTM grid covers from 80° S to 84° N, four more degrees north than the U.S. system. Once again, the world is divided into sixty 6°-wide zones, beginning at the IDL and increasing in number east back to the IDL.

But in addition to the numbered grid zones, the international UTM system divides the world into 8°-tall zones of latitude, beginning at 80°. Each of these zones receives a letter from "C" to "X," (the letters "I" and "O" are omitted since they can easily be confused with the numbers "1" and "0"). Therefore, in the international version, a UTM coordinate includes a numbered zone and a lettered zone—11 X, for example—and then the easting and northing as in the U.S. system.

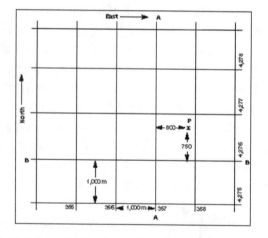

The first figure depicts the numbered UTM grid zones in the continental United States. Calculating a UTM coordinate is simple. Point "P" on the second figure is found by measuring the number of meters east and north of the principle 1,000-meter grid lines bounding it. As shown, "P" lies 800 meters east of grid line "A" and 750 meters north of grid line "B." *(Courtesy of USGS)*

In the international system each grid can be broken down once more, by dividing each grid zone into 100,000-meter squares. Starting from the southwest corner of each zone the grid is lettered "north" and "east" from "A" to "G." This further delineation is not shown on Geocaching.com and is rarely used outside the military, but it's important to be aware of. Thus, a complete international UTM coordinate would appear as: 10 S ES $^{56}$7890E $^{42}$78913N, yet most of the time, and for our purposes, this same coordinate would appear as 10 S 567890E 4278913N.

Reading a UTM coordinate from a map is much simpler than reading a Lat/Lon coordinate and does not require any complicated math. Begin reading a UTM coordinate by finding which zone the map is in. This can be found in the bottom left on USGS topographic maps or in the "GPS Waypoints & Coordinates" sections on newer Trails Illustrated maps. Keep in mind that most U.S.-produced maps do not have the alphabetical grid letter from the international system; to determine this you will need to count the 8° grid zones from 80° south through the equator to the latitude of your map. Most of the United States falls inside row "S" from 32° N to 40° N.

Once you've found your zone, look at the bottom right-hand corner your map and locate the easting in the marginalia, usually shown in blue type. It will read something like $^{4}$35$^{000}$E and, reading from right to left across the bottom neatline, will descend. Locate your point of interest and, on the marginalia, the two eastings that it lies between. Remember that dissimilar to Lat/Lon, UTM uses a square metric grid. Thus, finding the easting can be "guesstimated," or precisely located by using any object and the scale bar printed on your map for distance measurement. Let's assume that your point lies between $^{4}$25 and $^{4}$30. If you map does not have a UTM grid overlaid upon it, use a ruler and carefully connect the tick marks and crosshairs on the map, as done with the Lat/Lon exercise. Next, using anything, even a twig if you must, place one end of it on the

grid line to the left of your point of interest and then mark its corresponding position to the right on your object. Then simply compare
this distance to the printed metric scale bar on your map. This
imprecise method will easily get you within 100 meters of the correct position, or only 300'. After estimating your easting, repeat the
same process, but instead use the northing grid. Northings will also
start at the bottom right of your map and increase heading north, or
up the page. Northings will appear as $^{44}05^{000m}$N, for example. Once
you've estimated your northing, you now have a complete UTM
coordinate of 13S $^{42}$5890E $^{44}$10250N.

To make life really easy for you, once again I strongly recommend investing a few dollars in a plastic map grid reader. Not only
will this make reading Lat/Lon coordinates easier, it makes reading
UTM coordinates a breeze and is highly accurate. You simply need
to place your UTM card in the bottom right-hand corner of the
intersection point of any two known UTM eastings and northings,
and then count the number of meters east and north of your point in
order to determine a position.

Finding your known position on a map is even easier. Once
again, begin at the bottom right-hand corner of your map and read
the eastings along the bottom edge to find the grid your desired
coordinate lies between. Next, read the northings along the right
edge of the map to narrow down the section you lie in. For precise
positioning, use an object and the scale bar in the same fashion you
would use to find a coordinate. But if you've become savvy reading
contour lines, assuming you are reading a topographic map, you
should be able to look at your surroundings and compare them to
the section of the map you are on and find your approximate location.

I plan all of my outdoor activities using software such as
National Geographic's TOPO! or a MapMachine kiosk. Both of these
tools, and others similar to them, enable you to overlay a UTM grid
directly onto your printed map, often with a grid spacing of your

choice. If you were to overlay a 200-meter grid on the map, you could easily estimate a position with accuracy, at minimum of 30 meters—if not better—without any tools at all.

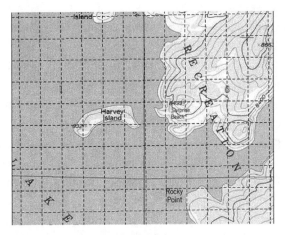

This image from National Geographic's TOPO! has a 200-meter UTM grid overlaid upon it. *(Map created with TOPO! © 2003 National Geographic Maps)*

I certainly don't want to tell you to give up Lat/Lon in place of UTM, but as you can see there are some significant advantages for a GPS user. Most of the GPS instruction books will reinforce the subtle message I've told here, but usually with more brute force by emphasizing that UTM is the *only* way to navigate. However, if you are comfortable with Lat/Lon it will work fine as well.

Another extremely important concept to understand is datum, and this is where a lot of first-time GPS users go wrong. Datum is defined as the fixed starting point for a coordinate system, but what exactly does that mean? Imagine if you were to construct a new coordinate system for the world, then the first thing you'd need to do is decide precisely where you'd like it to emanate from. This, of course, would be affected by the shape of the Earth as well, for while the world is round, it's actually more oblique rather than spherical.

The study of the Earth's shape and creating cartographic projections to best model it is a very complex mathematical operation, one that I cannot even begin to describe. But if you are looking for further answers, I suggest beginning your new college education with a degree in geodesy. In simple terms, each coordinate system—whether Lat/Lon, UTM, or other—can use any one of thousands of different types of datums, or starting points, for their projection. This is important to understand because if datums cross, from map to map or from map to GPS, you will find yourself in the wrong place. For outdoor recreationists this is a real challenge. Nearly all USGS topographic maps on store shelves today were created using the NAD27 mapping datum, which stands for North American Datum of 1927. However, some newer USGS quads, and most new cartography, are now produced in NAD83/WGS84 (North American Datum of 1983/World Geodetic System of 1984). Your GPS receiver was automatically set to the default mapping datum of NAD83/WGS84, but if you read a coordinate from a USGS topo, as done in our previous exercises, chances are it will be in NAD27. If you were to use this coordinate without changing your datum settings on your GPS prior to imputing it, you'd find yourself at least a city block away from where you intended to be. Things could get worse. You could be using the Old Hawaiian Datum or the Ancient Egyptian Datum.

Luckily, most new maps, such as those by Trails Illustrated, Green Trails, and others, include coordinates in NAD83/WGS84 and save us from this problem. Even the USGS is beginning to update the 7.5-minute topos to this new standard. For those of us who use software, online services, or kiosks for our maps, nearly all of these are, by default, NAD83/WGS84, including coordinates provided on Geocaching.com. But, once again, it is very important to start using any map by reading the marginalia, and this is where you'll find what datum the coordinates are provided in. If you find that they are different from the datum of your GPS, simply set your receiver to the datum of the map that you are using and then enter the coordinate you've determined from the map. GPS receivers, and most software programs, are smart enough to convert these coordinates to another datum when you change the GPS preference back to NAD83/WGS84 or another. But keep in mind that you'll always want your GPS and the map you are using in the field working from the same datum or you'll find yourself lost.

## Basic Functions of GPS Receivers

With your new understanding of coordinate systems and datums there are some basic GPS concepts to apply. As we all know, GPS receivers calculate our position, and when supplied with a position or coordinate of another location they can direct us on how to get there, as in the case of locating a geocache. Each GPS manufacturer puts a spin on how this action occurs and the set of features and functions that their models include, but a couple basic traits are common to most receivers: waypoints, routes, and tracks.

A waypoint is simply another name for a position or specific place. When you reach the trailhead of your next hike and you select the "mark" button on your GPS, you are, in fact, saving your current position as a waypoint. When you manually input the position of the geocache you are trying to find, its position is a waypoint. Depending on the robustness of your GPS receiver's memory, it can hold hundreds to thousands of waypoints in its library. Then, navigating to a waypoint is as easy as selecting one from the list stored on your receiver and entering "go to."

Navigating in this fashion, from a place to a singular waypoint, is often not practical due to terrain, buildings, or other obstacles. Therefore, we find that navigating via GPS receivers is done by following a string of waypoints, known as a route. Just as you wouldn't drive from your house to the grocery store in a straight line, you won't hike, paddle, or bike from the trailhead to a campsite in a straight line either. Instead, you'll want to go from one point to a place where a major change in direction is encountered and so on until you reach your destination. To do this, you'll first need to create a set of waypoints at each of these "intersections." In the grocery store example think of this as waypoints for your house, for the intersection at the end of your street, for the next street you turn on, for the road to the grocery store, and then the parking lot of the shop. The same principle applies in the outdoors, with waypoints commonly being created at trailheads, trail junctions, or other key landmarks as a means of making sure you are on the right path. Creating a route in your GPS is as simple as selecting a set of waypoints in the sequence you want to travel to them. Once again, routes vary by receiver; some units are able to hold a few, while others can hold dozens. Routes are generally able to contain twenty or so waypoints, but again, this varies. When following a route, your GPS will point you in the direction of travel to the first waypoint on the list, and when you reach that waypoint it will automatically go to the second, and so on. Some receivers also give you the option to reverse a route, taking you back the exact way you came. For geocache hunts that require navigating through large parks or take you on long hikes, routes are a great way to quickly and accurately navigate.

Tracks are another useful GPS feature. Most GPS receivers create a "track log," a figurative breadcrumb trail of your positions. The track features on a GPS receiver can be programmed to record your position at set intervals, perhaps every minute or every ten minutes. Tracks create digital records of how you got to where you are, and in the worst case scenario they can lead you back to where you started. Beyond the safety net that a track log creates, it can be used as a great mapping tool for those with some of the topographic mapping software. By setting the time intervals at which your GPS receiver creates an entry into the track log to best suit your means of transportation, your GPS will create a highly accurate map of the trail or path you've traveled. For example, you can set your GPS to track less frequently when walking at a slow pace and more often when riding a bike. The software packages will allow you to automatically load and display this log on top of the topo data, thereby creating your very own up-to-date map. In fact, most professional cartographers and agencies such as the U.S. Forest Service use this feature of GPS units for precisely this function, enabling them to create highly accurate maps of roads, trails, and points of interest.

Beyond geocaching, I find my GPS most useful as a tool for recording my outdoor adventures. Along with some mapping software I've created a set of journals for my activities. One contains all of my fly-fishing trips, showing places I've caught fish and a quick note of what fly I used, the time of day, etc. Another journal details my mountain biking trails, and I use yet another for hiking and one for snowshoeing. Now I can easily share places to go and things to do with friends, just as easily as learning about a new geocache, simply by providing them with a set of waypoints or a custom map generated from my track logs.

## Map Scale, Distances, and Working with a Compass

Scale and calculating distance on a map go hand in hand. The scale at which a map is created determines how much detail can be shown in relation to its sheet size. Scale can be expressed in several ways, either graphically, as a ratio, or by statement. A graphical scale bar usually depicts distance on a map through a simple image similar to a ruler. Dissimilar to either a ratio or a statement, only a graphic scale bar will remain accurate if the entire map is photocopied and reduced or enlarged in size by a certain percentage. A ratio scale is often shown in the form of 1:24000, in which the number before the colon refers to any unit of measurement on the map and number after the colon refers to the number of same units it would equal in the real world. In the scale of 1:24000, the standard scale of USGS 7.5-minute series topographic maps, 1" on the map equals 24,000" on Earth, or a little less than 4/10ths of a mile. The final means to represent scale is through a statement, such as "1" equals 1 mile."

Thus, calculating distance on a map begins by finding and understanding the map's scale. Assuming the map you are using has a scale bar, it is very easy to calculate the distance between two points in a straight line; it entails positioning any straight object between the two points and then comparing that to the scale bar, which usually displays a variety of distance units. But for maps with ratios or stated scales only, calculating the distance between two points requires some basic math and a ruler. You'll also want to memorize that there are 63,360 inches, or 5,280 feet, in one mile. With these two numbers you should be able to perform any basic computations necessary in order to understand map distance in relation to Earth distance.

While measuring straight line distances may be helpful for determining how far off an object is, it is usually more realistic to measure the distance of a curved line, perhaps of a trail or road. A simple trick to accomplish this is to use a blank sheet of paper and a sharp pencil. Create a starting mark on one edge of the sheet and then line it up with the beginning of the curved line you wish to measure. Make another mark at the point where the line curves, but do not lift your pencil from the sheet. Instead, use it as a fulcrum to pivot the sheet to line up with the next straight portion of the line, and then repeat. Continue this process of marking, pivoting, and realigning until you reach the end of your curved line. On the edge of your sheet you now have a straightened version of your curved line. Simply measure this distance with a ruler or compare to a scale bar and you're done.

The final concept in land navigation that we should focus on is finding and understanding directions using a map and compass. Being proficient at this age-old means of navigation will not only improve your geocaching ability from a planning and finding sense, it will also provide you with the confidence to safely navigate anywhere in the world.

The basic unit of measurement for land navigation is the degree (°), and when working with a map and compass a specific degree is referred to as an azimuth. There are 360 degrees in a circle and they are measured from 0°, or north. The four cardinal directions—north, south, east, and west—lie at 0°, 180°, 90°, and 270° respectively.

To read an azimuth between two points on a map you'll need a protractor and, in some cases, your compass may have one built into the baseplate. Begin by drawing a precise, straight line between the two points. Next, place your protractor on the starting point "1"; be certain that it lines up to the index point of your protractor (the small black line) on the mark and that your protractor is parallel to lines of latitude and perpendicular to lines of longitude on the map. Finally, read the degree that corresponds to your drawn line (depending on your protractor this may be an inner or outer ring of numbers).

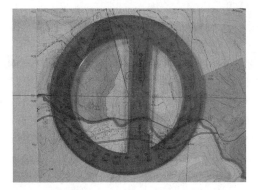

Carefully align your protractor using lines of latitude on your map. In this example the protractor is aligned using the 55' parallel on the map and the 270° and 90° marks on the instrument. The bearing in this example is 345°, uncorrected for magnetic declination. *(Photograph by Mike Dyer)*

If you want to determine your bearing to return from point "2" to "1" without your protractor, you can apply some simple math to calculate a "back azimuth." To determine a back azimuth you either add or subtract 180° from your first azimuth. If your original azimuth is less than 180° then you add 180° to that number. If the original azimuth is greater than 180° then you subtract. Let's assume that in our example the determined azimuth from point "1" to "2" is 93°. Therefore the calculated back azimuth would be 273°.

In the examples above we have determined bearings directly from the map. However, when in the field we'll utilize a compass. Compasses point to magnetic north (MN). However, there are two other "norths" that play a critical role in working with a map and compass: true north (TN) and grid north (GN), both of which are noted in the compass rose on a USGS topographic map. MN lies in northern Canada where there are great concentrations of iron ore. TN is the North Pole, where all lines of longitude converge. Finally, GN is the direction that all vertical lines in UTM point. Here in the United States GN is rarely used and is often misconstrued with either lines of TN or MN; but elsewhere in the world, TN is rarely used.

Consequently, when using a compass it is important to note the variations between what your compass is pointing to (magnetic north) and either true or grid north. The variation in location between magnetic north and either grid or true north is technically referred to as declination and is represented in degrees. Nearly every map contains a diagram that shows declination as an arrow and its associated direction either east or west of TN or GN, along with the date when the declination was calculated. Believe it or not, magnetic declination is slowly changing; therefore, if you use an old map and old declination information you will incorrectly navigate by compass.

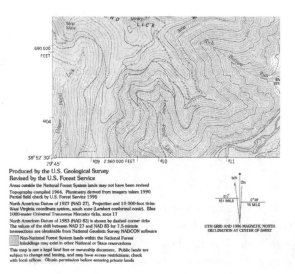

Produced by the U.S. Geological Survey
Revised by the U.S. Forest Service
Areas outside the National Forest System lands may not have been revised
Topography compiled 1964. Planimetry derived from imagery taken 1990
Partial field check by U.S. Forest Service 1995
North American Datum of 1927 (NAD 27). Projection and 10 000-foot ticks:
West Virginia coordinate system, south zone (Lambert conformal conic). Blue
1000-meter Universal Transverse Mercator ticks, zone 17
North American Datum of 1983 (NAD 83) is shown by dashed corner ticks
The values of the shift between NAD 27 and NAD 83 for 7.5-minute
intersections are obtainable from National Geodetic Survey NADCON software
Non-National Forest System lands within the National Forest
Inholdings may exist in other National or State reservations
This map is not a legal land line or ownership document. Public lands are
subject to change and leasing, and may have access restrictions; check
with local offices. Obtain permission before entering private lands

UTM GRID AND 1996 MAGNETIC NORTH
DECLINATION AT CENTER OF SHEET

In this image from a USGS quadrangle in West Virginia,
the declination diagram shows a magnetic north declination 8.5° west of true north (shown as a star). Grid north is
shown to be 0.5° east of true north. *(Courtesy of USGS)*

If you calculated an azimuth using a protractor, you will need to
adjust this bearing mathematically in order to use it with your compass. In Colorado, for example, magnetic declination is currently 10°
E. If I calculated a map azimuth of 100° using a protractor, I would
need to subtract 10° from this azimuth in order to compensate for
the fact that my compass will direct me on a course overly to the
right. If I were elsewhere in the world and the declination was 10° W
from TN, then I would need to add 10° to my map azimuth in order
to compensate for being directed overly left.

Converting an azimuth obtained by a compass back to a map
azimuth works in the opposite way. If the declination on your map is
pointing to the east, then add the declination factor to your magnetic azimuth. If the declination on your map is pointing to the west,
then subtract the declination factor from your magnetic azimuth.

Using a compass is easy, and every model comes with a basic set of instructions that I encourage you to read. General operation consists of taking a bearing to an object and navigating on a known azimuth, say, for example, one determined from a map or provided to you in an offset cache or multicache.

Taking a bearing to an object is a simple as holding the compass in front of you, level with the ground, and using the sight or index mark on the baseplate to aim your compass directly at the object. Next, turn the azimuth bezel on your compass (numbered from 0° to 360°) until the orienting arrow matches up perfectly with the north side of the compass needle (usually red). Finally, keeping the compass aimed at your object, read the azimuth that intersects with the index point at the top of your compass; this is the magnetic azimuth to that object.

Having aimed the compass at the tree in this image, the bezel on the compass was rotated until the orienting arrows and the magnetic needle were aligned and the exact bearing of 5° could be read. *(Photograph by Mike Dyer)*

Following a prescribed magnetic azimuth is even simpler. First, turn the azimuth ring on your compass until the magnetic bearing you wish to follow matches with the index point. Next, holding the compass level with the ground and in front of you, turn your body until the north magnetic arrow lines up with the orienting lines in the compass bezel. You are now facing in the prescribed direction. Following this azimuth is now as simple as walking in a straight line, verifying your track by keeping the magnetic needle and orienting arrows aligned. To navigate accurately and safely, once you've aligned our compass, the best practice is to note a distant object that lies exactly in your intended path of travel. Hike to this object and then take an additional bearing from this point versus attempting to negotiate terrain while constantly reading your compass.

With these basic skills perfected, using your map and compass in the field to determine your position is simple. One of the most useful skills to have as a hiker is resection, or plotting your location on a map by determining your position from at least two other objects you can see in the real world and on your map. Imagine you are standing in a huge open meadow and on your horizon are two summits that you can clearly distinguish on your map. You can find your exact position on the map by using your compass and taking a bearing to each of those summits. The steps to completing an accurate resection are

1 Locate two features in the real world that you can accurately locate on your map.
2 Using your compass, determine the magnetic azimuth to each feature on the ground and then convert this number to its map azimuth by adding or subtracting based on declination.
3 Calculate the back azimuth for each of the map azimuths by adding or subtracting 180°.
4 Using your protractor, place it on each of the objects and mark their back azimuths.

5 Carefully draw a line from each point until they intersect; this is your position.

A very "down and dirty" form of resection can be used if you are traveling on a known linear object, for example, a trail or road. By taking only one bearing to a distant object and using the road or trail marked on your map as the second intersection point from your calculated reverse map azimuth, you can easily determine your approximate location. This can be handy when hiking a long trail and wanting to quickly get a sense of your progress or proximity to camp. It can also be a fun way of learning the names of features you see in the distance when traveling by car or by plane.

In reverse, the skill of resection can be used to locate an object on a map by taking bearings from two or more positions. This process is known as intersection. For our purposes as outdoor enthusiasts this is much less useful, but is used frequently by rescue personnel and the U.S. Forest Service in fire lookout towers. Assuming you have people in different locations, they can each take a bearing to an object—for example, a forest fire—and from their separate locations determine and plot the azimuths on a map. Just as in resection, where the plotted lines converge is the location of the object. In our example, it's a mysterious plume of smoke.

With map reading, GPS, and compass skills any adventurer can navigate safely and accurately across all types of terrain and over extreme distances. Although not necessary while geocaching it's helpful in order to preserve battery life in your GPS during a long backcountry trip. This can be accomplished by using your GPS to verify your position, plot it on a map, and then navigate by azimuths until you feel it wise to once again power your GPS back on and reconfirm your location.

While geocaching, your expertise with these three essential tools for navigation will increase your ability to find the toughest caches, and it will enable you to create unique cache games based on your skill. I hope that the fun and excitement you've experienced while geocaching has awoken your spirit of adventure and piqued your interest in the outdoors and navigation.

# Appendix A
## Geocache Resources

**Web sites where you can find geocaches, letterboxes, maps, and other useful information relating to the sport of geocaching:**

**www.geocaching.com**

Geocaching.com is the official site for the geocache game worldwide.

**www.letterboxing.org**

Letterboxing.org is the official site for the sport of letterboxing in North America.

**www.mapblast.com**

Operated by Microsoft, the Mapblast search engine provides most of the maps found on Geocaching.com.

**www.randmcnally.com**

Known for their road atlases and paper maps, Rand McNally's Web site offers point-to-point driving directions and travel planning tools.

**www.nationalgeographic.com/mapmachine**

National Geographic's recently redesigned online MapMachine has a free searchable database of topographic maps and aerial photos for the United States, along with a wide selection of atlas maps and unique layers for places worldwide.

**www.offroute.com**

Offroute.com operates a seamless topographic map database for the entire United States from which users can order high quality prints. Offroute also offers a vast array of GPS receivers, software, and books via their online store.

## www.mapquest.com

Mapquest.com has online road maps and travel planning databases that are great for finding your way to the trailhead of any cache, no matter how far from home.

## www.usgs.gov

The USGS has a vast array of map resources online in the geography section. Free information includes topographic map symbols, how-to guides, and searchable databases for map names and content.

**Manufacturers of consumer-based GPS receivers:**

## Garmin

www.garmin.com

Garmin designs and manufactures an extensive selection of GPS receivers for outdoor enthusiasts, aviators, and mariners alike. Some of their latest models include features designed specifically for geocaching. Their Web site contains model-by-model comparisons and information on what is, and how to use, GPS technology.

## Magellan

www.magellangps.com

Thales Navigation is one of the world's leading developers and manufacturers of positioning, navigational, and guidance equipment with global operations. Thales Navigation markets its Magellan-brand GPS solutions in the consumer electronics, recreation, and automotive markets and its GPS and global navigation satellite system (GNSS) professional products in the survey, geographic information systems (GIS)/mapping, and original equipment manufacturer (OEM) markets. Through its joint venture with Hertz, Thales Navigation has developed the Hertz NeverLost® vehicle navigational system. Thales Navigation's key innovations include the first U.S. commercial handheld GPS receiver for positioning and navigation, and the first handheld GPS with industry standard secure digital memory card capabilities.

## Suunto

www.suunto.com

Suunto USA: 1-800-543-9124

Suunto Canada: 1-800-776-7770

Suunto manufacturers a vast array of equipment for outdoor enthusiasts and geocachers, including the X9 GPS-enabled wrist-top computer, as well as other feature-packed electronic instruments and precision compasses.

## Brunton

www.brunton.com

Brunton manufacturers technologically advanced optical instruments, Global Positioning Systems, portable power products, high-performance cook stoves, educational kits, and dealer support displays. This unmistakable variety, affordability, and quality keeps Brunton's name in the minds of outdoor enthusiasts and professionals.

**Map publishers:**

## National Geographic Maps

www.nationalgeographic.com/maps

1-800-962-1643

From the trail to the universe, National Geographic has the map you need. National Geographic Maps is the publisher and provider of a wide variety of mapping products including TOPO! digital mapping products and accessories, MapMachine Kiosks, Trails Illustrated trail maps, city and state travel maps, road atlases, international Adventure Maps, reference maps, and globes.

## Maptech, Inc.

www.maptech.com

1-888-839-5551

Maptech offers PC, Pocket PC, and Palm software for planning and real-time GPS positioning on USGS topo maps. It also offers a free "Mapserver" at www.maptech.com. The Mapserver is a good resource for viewing topo maps on the Web.

## DeLorme

www.delorme.com

1-800-561-5105

Located in Yarmouth, Maine, DeLorme has more than twenty-five years of cartographic and software experience and more than 125 employees dedicated to creating the best in mapping, GIS, and GPS products. DeLorme digital products are rooted in the DeLorme XMap development platform, which is scalable for future growth and endorsed by millions of dedicated digital mapping software users worldwide. DeLorme adheres to the principal of investing in innovative technology to generate affordable and easy-to-use navigational and mapping products.

## USGS

www.usgs.gov

The USGS serves the nation by providing reliable scientific information to describe and understand the Earth; minimize loss of life and property from natural disasters; manage water, biological, energy, and mineral resources; and enhance and protect our quality of life.

**Easy step-by-step checklists:**

**Getting Started in Geocaching Shopping List**

## The essentials:
- ❑ GPS receiver
- ❑ Internet access
- ❑ Compass (either baseplate, lensatic, or mirrored)
- ❑ Maps of the area where you intend to geocache
    - ❑ Road maps for getting to the trailhead
    - ❑ Topographic/trail maps for getting to the cache
- ❑ First-aid kit

## Nonessential suggested items:
- ❑ Protective bag for GPS receiver
- ❑ Computer-to-GPS cable
- ❑ Topographic mapping software

**Finding Your First Cache in Ten Simple Steps:**

1  Go to Geocaching.com, type in your zip code, and display a list of caches in your area.

2  Select the cache you wish to find and print out its page.

3  Use maps provided on the cache page to get the general location of where the cache is hidden (what park, which town, etc.).

4  Get driving directions to the park, if necessary, by using an online map tool or road map of the area.

5  Locate the closest park access point to the cache and determine which trails to take to get to the cache by using a topographic map or other park map.

6  Load the coordinates of the cache into your GPS, but ensure that your receiver is set to the appropriate datum first (WGS84).

7  Once at the trailhead, turn on your GPS receiver and wait for a signal, then have your GPS "go to" your stored cache location. Don't forget that your GPS may not point you in the right direction unless you are moving.

8  Stay on trails as much as possible until you must go off trail to locate the cache.

9  Use your GPS to define the search area of the cache.

10  Once you've located the cache, sign the logbook, trade items if you wish, and then return home to log your find on the Web site.

**Hiding Your First Cache in Ten Simple Steps:**

1 Decide which type of cache game you'd like to create.

2 Choose how large your cache will be. This may be dictated by the size of the hiding spot you have in mind and whether or not you want to trade items in your cache.

3 Acquire a durable container for your cache, as well as a logbook, notification letter, pen, and any other trinkets you wish to place in the cache.

4 Mark the outside of your cache in permanent marker with "Geocache, do not remove," along with the date it was placed and its nickname.

5 Go to your intended hiding spot; verify that your location is not in an "illegal" cache location and that it will not disturb the natural environment.

6 Hide your cache and, if necessary, use rocks, downed branches, or other materials to conceal the cache from plain view. Remember, good cache hiding spots are found, not made.

7 Acquire an accurate signal with your GPS and mark the cache's position. Make sure that your datum is correctly set on your GPS (to WGS84).

8 Verify that the position is accurate by walking away and then using your GPS to navigate back to the cache; re-mark the cache position if necessary.

9 Return home with your accurate coordinate and fill out the appropriate online form for hiding a new cache, including game type, cache size, coordinate, descriptions, and your spoiler.

10 Your cache submission will be reviewed and posted to the Internet within a few days. Remember, you are now responsible for maintaining your cache.

**Finding a Latitude/Longitude Coordinate on a USGS Map
in Ten Simple Steps:**

1 Read the marginalia of the map to ensure that you understand the scale, how recently the map was created, contour
interval, and coordinate systems displayed on the map.

2 Using a ruler and a sharp pencil, carefully connect the tick
marks and intersection marks (+) of the latitude and longitude lines, dividing the map into nine sections. Each section
should be 2.5' in size.

3 Carefully mark the point of interest you wish to find the
coordinate for with a sharp pencil.

4 Using a centimeter ruler, place the "o" mark on the line of
latitude below your mark and then angle the ruler so that the
"30-cm" mark lines up with the line of latitude above your mark.

5 Keeping the "o" and "30" marks on the lines of latitude, slide
the ruler to the left of right until it lines up with your point
of interest. Read the centimeter mark that corresponds to
its position.

6 Multiply the number read from the centimeter ruler by five
to equal the number of seconds to add to the latitude line
below the point of interest.

7 Using the same technique as described above, line up the ruler
on the two lines of longitude that bracket your point of interest.

8 Slide the ruler so that your point of interest corresponds to a
mark on the centimeter ruler; read its value.

9 Multiply the determined value by five to equal the number of
seconds of longitude to add to the longitude line to the right
of your point of interest.

10 Complete your calculations for latitude and longitude, bearing
in mind that there are sixty minutes in a degree and sixty
seconds in a minute.

**Finding a UTM Position on a USGS Topographic Map
in Ten Simple Steps:**

1 Locate the zone number of your map and the blue Universal
  Transverse Mercator (UTM) tick marks along the map's neatline. On a USGS quad this is the in-paragraph in the bottom
  left-hand corner of the map.

2 Locate your point of interest and connect the four tick marks
  that surround it.

3 Find the easting coordinate in the bottom right-hand corner
  of the map displayed in the format: $^6 19^{000}$E.

4 Read the tick marks across the bottom of the map and find
  the two ticks that frame your point of interest.

5 Using the metric scale bar at the bottom of the map or a grid
  tool, measure the number of meters from the grid line to the
  left of your point and add these to that line's value. For
  example, if the line is $^6 13$ and you measure 150 meters, the
  easting would be $^6 13^{150}$E.

6 Repeat this same process, beginning in the bottom right-
  hand corner with the northing, displayed as $^{43} 04^{000m}$N.

7 Read up the right margin and find the two northing lines
  that frame your point of interest.

8 Using your ruler and metric scale bar on the bottom of the
  map, or a grid tool, measure the meters from the line below
  your point to it.

9 Add the distance to the line. For example, let's assume you
  measured and calculated 635 meters. The northing will be
  displayed as $^{43} 04^{635m}$N.

10 Put the zone from the marginalia together with your calculated easting and northing to create the final UTM coordinate.

## Glossary of Terms

**Azimuth:** most commonly, the length in degrees measured from true north; a precise direction measured in degrees

**Back Azimuth:** the opposite direction of an azimuth; precisely 180 degrees in the opposite direction of travel

**Baseplate:** referring to a baseplate compass; a compass with a see-through base, usually made of clear plastic, which contains useful map reading and interpretation tools such as scales and distance conversion information

**Benchmark:** A mark of height that has been determined by spirit leveling, a surveying method; commonly, a benchmark is seen in the field as an engraving or an affixed brass plaque.

**Cache:** pronounced "cash"; a box containing supplies or provisions. In the case of geocaching, a cache is the object of the game. It is a container that contains a logbook and, typically, items for trade.

**Contour Interval:** the vertical change between consecutive contour lines, typically in feet or meters

**Contour Line:** a line on a map that joins places of equal height and, sometimes, equal depth. Contour lines are commonly found on topographic maps and are shown as brown or black lines.

**Coordinate:** a point referenced on a grid by X and Y axes drawn at right angles to each other

**Datum:** the fixed starting point of a scale or coordinate system

**Degree:** the measure of distance in a circle from its starting point; a circle contains 360 degrees

**Estimated Point Error (EPE):** a generated value for the accuracy of the current position your GPS is reporting

**Geocoin:** a coin that contains a unique ID and is traded from geocache to geocache; similar to a Travel Bug, its whereabouts are tracked on the Internet.

**Global Positioning System (GPS):** a system developed by the military for providing accurate navigational information in all weather and terrain conditions; GPS utilizes a constellation of satellites to beam signals to Earth that GPS receivers decode to reveal their current position on Earth.

**Grid North:** the direction in which meridians in the Universal Transverse Mercator (UTM) coordinate system point

**Index Contour:** typically every fourth or fifth contour line, shown in heavier type and includes a printed numeric value

**International Date Line (IDL):** a line of longitude located at 180°

**Kiosk:** a freestanding point of purchase display, typically electronic and self-service

**Large Cache:** a size of a geocache container, typically equivalent to a five-gallon bucket

**Latitude:** imaginary lines drawn around the Earth parallel to the equator; lines of latitude range from 0° found at the equator to 90° at either Pole

**Leave No Trace (LNT):** a nonprofit organization with principles that encourage thoughtful, low-impact use of public places and wilderness

**Lensatic:** referring to a lensatic compass; a lensatic compass has two sights designed to aid in taking accurate bearings to distant objects.

**Letterboxing:** a game similar to geocaching founded in the United Kingdom; letterboxing involves hiding boxes that contain a specific rubber stamp. When a letterboxer locates the box he or she stamps their personal logbooks with the stamp in the box and stamps the box's logbook with their own personal stamp.

**Logbook:** a requirement for nearly all cache games. A logbook is typically as simple as a small pad or notebook; people who locate a cache sign the logbook as proof of their discovery.

**Longitude:** imaginary lines that run at right angles to lines of latitude and encircle the globe. Longitude is measured in degrees, ranging from 0° to 180° east and west of the Prime Meridian (0°), which runs through Greenwich, England.

**Magnetic Declination:** the variance in degrees between true north and magnetic north caused by the Earth's magnetic field

**Magnetic North:** the direction in which a compass points; a

location in northern Canada

**Marginalia:** the key information contained on the margins of all maps

**Meridian:** a line of longitude

**Microcache:** referring to the size of the cache; microcaches are typically the size of a 35-mm film canister.

**Minute:** a measurement of distance and a division of one degree; there are sixty minutes in one degree and sixty seconds in one minute.

**Mirrored:** referring to a mirrored compass; a mirrored compass uses a mirror, which enables the user to sight a distant object and accurately read its bearing at the same time.

**Multicache:** a geocache game in which more than one cache box must be found in sequence in order to locate the final cache

**Mystery Cache:** a geocache game that typically involves solving a complex puzzle or riddle in order to learn the geographic directions to the final cache location

**Neatline:** the boundary drawn around the outside of a map, which has an exact relation to a particular coordinate system

**North American Datum of 1927 (NAD27):** the datum in which most USGS topographic maps are created and, more importantly, the datum that is not the default on most GPS receivers, software, or maps produced by kiosks

**North American Datum of 1983 (NAD83):** a later, more accurate datum, identical to World Geodetic Survey 1984 (WGS84) and the default datum on Geocaching.com, GPS receivers, mapping software, and mapping kiosks

**North Arrow:** one of several arrows typically contained in a compass rose. A north arrow points toward the North Pole. In a compass rose, the north arrow is the tallest and usually points toward a star symbol.

**Offset Cache:** a geocache game in which the user must decipher information from a landmark such as a plaque, sign, or marker as a means of learning the geographic coordinate to the final cache location

**Orienting Arrow:** an arrow or set of lines contained inside a compass bezel designed for aligning with the magnetic needle of the compass for determining a bearing

**Parallel:** another name for a line of latitude

**Quad:** a common shorthand name for a quadrangle typically associated with a USGS 7.5-minute topographic map

**Regular Cache:** a regular cache can be one of two things: 1.) referring to the traditional geocaching game in which the seeker is provided with the coordinate to a hidden cache and must find it; and 2.) the size of a cache box. A regular cache is the most common cache box size, typically an ammo box or plastic container, roughly eight inches by eight inches in size.

**Resection:** the orienting practice of using at least two distinct landmarks visible to the naked eye and discernable on a map to locate your position by a means of plotting bearings to them and then triangulating your position

**Reverse Cache:** a type of geocache game, sometimes known as a "locationless" cache; a reverse cache does not have a typical cache box but instead directs you to locate objects of a certain type and post coordinates to those positions as proof of finding them.

**Route:** in geocaching and GPS terminology, a route is a string or set of sequential coordinates, or waypoints, that lead you from point "A" to point "B"; a route is typically no more than twenty waypoints.

**Scale:** a level of representation; traditionally, this has applied to cartography, where scale is the ratio between map distance and on-the-ground distance.

**Second:** referring to the geographic measurement of distance and symbolized by the mark: ". There are sixty seconds in one degree minute, and there are sixty minutes in one degree.

**Selective Availability (SA):** Degradation of GPS signals. SA was removed in 2000 by presidential order and there are currently no plans to reinstate it; SA limited consumer-based GPS receivers to accuracy of roughly fifteen meters.

**Take Nothing Leave Nothing (TNLN):** a common acronym used by geocachers to describe the act of taking nothing from the cache and leaving nothing in return

**Take Nothing Leave Nothing Signed Log (TNLNSL):** a common acronym used by geocachers to describe the act of taking nothing from the cache and leaving nothing in the cache, but signing the logbook as proof of your find

**Topographic Map:** a map that shows the natural and human features of the Earth's surface within scale and correct relationship to one another; commonly, topographic maps use contour lines to depict the shape of the Earth in three dimensions.

**Traditional Cache:** a type of geocache game, sometimes known as either a basic or regular cache; a traditional cache game involves finding a cache box from a provided coordinate.

**Transit:** a professional model of compass or surveying instrument; transits provide highly accurate means of measuring bearings and angles.

**Travel Bug:** a dog tag–like device that is placed in a geocache; its whereabouts are then tracked via the Internet.

**True North:** true north is in the direction of the North Pole.

**Universal Transverse Mercator (UTM):** a coordinate system based on a metric grid; a UTM coordinate is read in terms of zone, easting, and northing.

**Virtual Cache:** a cache game in which the seeker locates an extraordinary place or view via a provided coordinate; a virtual cache gets its name from the fact that it does not have a cache box.

**Waypoint:** in geocaching and GPS terminology this refers to a singular location expressed in terms of a geographic coordinate.

**Webcam Cache:** a type of geocache game in which the seeker must travel to a particular coordinate where a webcam will take his or her picture. To complete the cache, the seeker must retrieve the picture from the Internet and e-mail it to the cache creator.

**Web site:** a location on the Internet with a set of pages that contain particular information

**Wide Area Augmentation Service (WAAS):** a radio-based system of transmitters scattered throughout the United States that provides an additional set of GPS signals to improve accuracy of GPS receivers. WAAS is available on select GPS receivers and is a free service to the users with the correct equipment.

**World Geographic Survey of 1984 (WGS84):** currently the most accepted datum; it is the equivalent to North American Datum of 1983 here in North America. WGS84 is the default datum on most GPS receivers, mapping software, and in-store kiosks.

**Zone:** an essential part of an UTM coordinate; in UTM, the Earth is divided into sixty zones of latitude, each 6° in width.

# Appendix B
# Bibliography

www.geocaching.com—provided information about the history of the sport, various types of games, rules and guidelines, and allowed usage of several screen shots

www.letterboxing.com—provided general information regarding the sport of letterboxing

www.usgs.gov—provided information on Universal Transverse Mercator (UTM), topographic maps, and general cartography

Brown, Lloyd A. *The Story of Maps*. Boston: Little Brown and Co., 1949.

Mayhew, Susan. *A Dictionary of Geography (Oxford Paperback Reference), Second Edition*. New York: Oxford Press, 1997.

National Geographic Maps. *Basic Map Skills Booklet*. Evergreen, Colo: National Geographic, 2003.

Small, George (Professor of Geography at San Francisco State University). *Geography 604 Course Reader*, 1999.

# Index

# About the Author

Mike Dyer has been a lifelong outdoor lover. At an early age he became involved in camping and other outdoor-related activities through Boy Scouts where he achieved the rank of Eagle Scout. Mike graduated from San Francisco State University with a dual degree in geography and business. Today Mike manages the MapMachine business unit for National Geographic and is an active committee member for International Map Trade Association (IMTA) and Volunteers for Outdoor Colorado (VOC). His strong mapping, technology, and navigation skills are the result of his classical education in geography and cartography, years of assisting customers with planning outdoor-related trips, and being at the forefront in navigation technology professionally. Mike lives in Evergreen, Colorado.